From the
Horse's Mouth

From the Horse's Mouth

A Memoir of San Francisco's Legendary
Iron Horse Restaurant, its charismatic
owner, and the Giorgetti family

Marilyn Pearsol Giorgetti

To order additional copies of this book, contact:
Xlibris Corporation
1-888-795-4274
www.Xlibris.com
Orders@Xlibris.com
27394

CONTENTS

Preface

T his is a true story. I am a horse. A famous horse. I lived in San Francisco in the marvelous heyday of rebirth after World War II from 1954 to 1973.

I was conceived and owned by a couple of upstarts named Sam and Leo, who thought they could outfox the President of Bank of America to get me started. They did!

All the infamous and notorious visited me and I was privy to the secrets of the world and a haven to those famous. There never was and never will be again a horse like me or times like those.

After marrying Leo, the charismatic owner of The Iron Horse Restaurant, and listening over time to him and his friends' tales of the adventures and shenanigans at The Horse, the people who visited there and why the great popularity, I felt compelled to document as much as I could to preserve its story if only as part of the history of San Francisco.

When I first proposed the idea of a book to Leo, he dismissed it saying it was his private life.

Then one evening in the spring of 2002, while having cocktails with Don Thornton, Joe Cotchett, and other friends at the historic San Benito Hotel in Half Moon Bay, Leo was again entertaining us with a happening at The Horse and I said as if like a mantra, "I still think it would make an interesting book." A chorus of "That's a great idea," or some such affirmation from the group seemed to lend some credence to my earlier suggestion. And this time I took heart from the fact that he did not dismiss the idea.

I let this seed germinate while I pondered the best method in which to write the story. First person would not do. Third person narrative appeared to be harboring on the boring.

One day in a split second it came to me: Let The Horse tell the story. As soon as I mentioned this to Leo, a smile spread across his face. "FROM THE HORSE'S MOUTH," he said.

I knew we were in business. He had sanctioned the re-telling.

Since we began openly discussing our endeavor, it was surprising to discover how many lives The Horse had impacted. It was impossible to document all the stories, anecdotes and historic moments of those experiencing them.

Behind the success of The Horse was the young, outgoing Italian owner, Leo Giorgetti, who, with his unique love of mankind, welcoming spirit, ingenuity and benevolence, created the atmosphere that enticed people from all over the world to return again and again. This is not to suggest that Sam Marconi, his partner, did not play a part in The Horse's success nor do I mean in any way to pay him less homage. Sam and Leo had been partners in two restaurants: The Iron Horse and Gold Street. Sam had been the driving force behind Gold Street, which was situated on a little alley off Montgomery Street.

Permission was given to use some authentic names. Otherwise names were changed but the events were accurate.

While Leo's name is mentioned abundantly in this story, I had intended a brief foray into his life. But, as the little recorder placed in front of Leo seemed to bring forth long forgotten anecdotes and interesting facts of his parents' lives, I decided to include more about the Giorgettis. Let us assume, then, that The Horse just knew of such things.

In Memory Of

Carl Wente—President, Bank of America
Who financed The Horse

Carl Rebman—Owner of the Shadows Restaurant
Who put it together to make the dream come true

Sam Marconi—Partner

Augie Mariucci—He brought life to The Horse

Ed Farrah—Original member of the Inner Circle

"I just wanted to go to America. It was the '50s and
Europe was still recovering from the war,
but America represented success,
represented power. It lit a fire in me."
—Arnold Schwarzenegger

Chapter One

THE HORSE WAS BORN

Oh, my God! The doors are opening! They're starting to come in. This is the beginning. I am alive!

At 5.00 p.m. on April 6, 1954, the doors of The Iron Horse opened not to close again until the year 2002. This was opening night and Leo and Sam had invited all the press and city officials.

If our enthused but nervous young hosts were at all concerned about people showing up for their party—after all, this opening was the make-or-break-gamble that would determine the future of The Horse—any fears were instantly dispelled upon opening the door to an eager, thirsty crowd waiting at #19 Maiden Lane. Leaning against the adjoining building in the direction of Union Square and Grant Street, with another group snaking toward the corner of Maiden Lane and Kearny Street, the crowd waited. Inasmuch as the *San Francisco Chronicle*, located at Fifth and Mission, and the *San Francisco Examiner*, located at Third and Market, were within walking distance, and the ad agencies were situated in the area, this was probably just a routine stop for them to drop in for a drink after work and check out the "New Kid on the Block." In addition the folks from television channels 2 and 5 joined the crowd. Having come right from work, most of the crowd was dressed comfortably and a relaxed atmosphere developed that set the tone for the rest of the evening.

Red-coated waiters, and waitresses dressed in black and white, made their way through the laughing and boisterous "know-everybody-crowd" trying to protect their trays of fried artichokes, zucchini fingers, meatballs, crab legs, and other delectable delicacies lavishly displayed, while enthusiastic guests leaning on the long bar, gripping tightly to their own drinks, were passing drinks to those not willing to risk their lives getting *up* to the bar.

Pedestrians on the street, not realizing it was a private party, were joining in the revelry.

As nine o'clock approached, which was to be the closing hour, Leo looked at Sam. Sam looked back at Leo and they both looked at the partygoers who had taken over the entire lounge and were stacked three deep at the bar. A light smokers' haze hovered lazily over their heads. Friends acknowledged each other from across the room. It was standing room only. Friendly gatherings were sighted in the dining area. Elegant dress mingled with loose ties hanging around necks. There was no denying the energy permeating the entire area.

"Whatta you think?" asked Leo.

"I don't know. Whatta *you* think?" Sam responded.

"Well, we have here all these ad people. We need them and they need us. We're into this ninety grand already, what's another two grand? I say, let'er rip."

So the doors stayed open and from that auspicious opening night and the ensuing great press, Leo and Sam never had to pay for advertising. They were ecstatic. After that night The Horse was never empty. I was born!

I became the darling of San Francisco. The meeting place. The place to be.

Why I was so popular and why I am remembered with nostalgia is simple:

PEOPLE experienced intimacy and happiness.

The Horse was a gathering spot not only for an occasional dinner or drink with a friend, but events like bridal showers, baby showers, weddings, receptions, first dates, marriage proposals, bachelor parties and anniversaries, were never-to-be-forgotten events to be stored in the heart. Many couples and groups of friends considered The Horse "their place." Many an intimate meal was shared here. It was only natural for folks to return again and again.

PEOPLE made The Horse what it was.

In those days, white gloves and hats were *de rigueur* for the ladies. They mingled at lunch, over martinis, right along with the martini-drinking businessmen. Ungloved and sans hats, the career gals joined this throng for a quick bite. My three chefs, three pantry men, two bartenders and a bar-boy never ceased in their preparation of food and dispensing drinks. The bartenders moved swiftly and efficiently keeping the nightly crowd well fueled and happy. The bar-boy stayed on his knees behind the bar. His sole responsibility was filling glasses with ice and keeping them ready for the bartenders to mix the drinks. The drink of the day was a martini and the price was 75 cents. Now that's a real martini, with gin, not today's vodka martini (although Herb Caen wanted to be different and tried his with vodka).

The glasses were so small that if the bartender put anything other than a small olive in the martini, the customer would say, "I didn't ask for salad." It took up too much gin room. So the rule was, always ask for an olive on the side. Heaven forbid you should get two olives in your glass.

No wonder we had fun: Each month we ordered 50 cases *each* of bourbon, vodka, scotch and gin. *Fifty cases!* Let's see . . . at twelve bottles to a case; that would equate to 2,400 bottles of liquor consumed at The Horse each month. That doesn't include the liqueurs or the wine.

The waiters appeared to be on roller skates balancing their savory loads. How they managed the stairs leading down to the beautifully appointed dining room to serve the hungry horde defies explanation.

Embracing all this, the jubilant 34-year-old Leo darted from one group to another like a hummingbird, the smile on his face growing by the minute. I was his baby and he was determined that I reach my full potential.

If you've never had the experience of visiting me, let me take you there: As you entered, passing under my prominent black bust, you'd see a colorful horizon of Czechoslovakian glass set above a facade of used brick.

Carl Rebman purchased my bust in far off romantic New Orleans then added six black hitching posts on the Lane.

My never-to-be-forgotten "Thanks" to Carl who waved his magic wand and enveloped me in the magnificence of Old World charm. (While Carl owned the Shadows Restaurant in San Francisco, his expertise in interior design was not generally well known). Wrought iron filigree railings and accents blended with wood-burned pine walls created a "been there a long time" look.

(I might interject here that Maiden Lane was originally named Morton Place. It evolved to Maiden Lane in the early 1900s in honor of the higher priced ladies of the night who plied their trade there.)

In all humility, to enter through my double doors into a cacophony of humanity was to realize that you have experienced a pulsing energy so vital that it propels you to stay, to visit, to take it all in.

Just inside, to the right past the long gleaming, mahogany bar, a stairway led you to the mezzanine, which was available for extra seating or a quiet haven for a visiting celebrity. This was also the location of Leo's office plus two banquet rooms and a service bar.

It was quite extraordinary to view the spacious and elegant interior from inside, since viewing The Horse from the outside gave the impression of a much smaller, but quaint, edifice.

There was a second set of double doors located farther down on Maiden Lane—the "back door" where one could rather discreetly enter and go through the kitchen or quietly ascend the stairs to the mezzanine. This was the route that Joe DiMaggio always took to the mezzanine. Joe would sit there in his solitude and have lunch or relax and read. It was his place of quietude and he came often.

Prior to my existence the restaurant was known as Solari's Grill. It was later renamed Frankie and Johnny's for a short time. It was during this interim, and at this location where Joe and Marilyn Monroe had their wedding reception on January 14th, 1954. Probably because of his nostalgia and because Leo honored his privacy, I became a haven for Joe. It was his turf.

Just to add a little intrigue here, I should tell you that there was also a secret entrance to The Horse situated in the rear on adjacent Kearny Street. It was located in a little cigar store. One could enter that establishment, go all the way to the back and behind a closed door—voila, a stairway to The Horse.

In front of The Horse, from the sidewalk to the left of the entrance, an elevator would periodically rise from beneath, topped by a rounded steel bar, exposing a yawning chasm that led to storage for all my supplies.

Small intimate rooms still existed above the restaurant when Leo and Sam bought me. They were converted into small private dining rooms for business people or whoever wanted to dine *a deux*.

To walk on my decadently plush carpet was to tread in the footsteps, and flirt with the ghosts, of not only Joe DiMaggio, but Maria Callas, Liberace, Pete Rozelle, George Christopher (mayor of San Francisco), Herb Caen and many more as you will see.

So it was in this vibrant ambiance that I came into being and started my life a mere nine years after the end of a world war. I was as ready as *they* were ready.

But let's go back. To understand me and why I'm so special, you have to know Leo.

The Iron Horse today with the front doors boarded.

Leo (l), an unidentified man, and Sam (r), at The Horse, 1956.

Leo and Sam at their Gold Street restaurant.

A typical standing-room-only crowd enjoy their evening at
The Horse.

(Photo courtesy of Allison Verfall)

Leo prepares drinks at the bar.

Chapter Two

LOVE STORY

I t all starts with Frederico Giorgetti and Maria Puccinelli, who were sweethearts in Lucca, Italy, in the early part of the 20th Century. The youngest of twelve children, Maria was born into a working class family, which was considered then to be well off. Frederico was a cooper. His manual dexterity resulted in perfect metal rings, which were then attached to the circumference of many wooden slats placed side by side, rounded slightly, to form a barrel; specifically wooden wine barrels.

Wanting to have a better life than the hard scrabble life in Italy at that time, they agreed that Frederico would travel to America and send for Maria when he had saved enough money. Frederico settled in Half Moon Bay, California, just south of San Francisco, where he accepted a foreman's position from a local farmer and produce shipper named John DeBenedetti, who grew artichokes and Brussels sprouts. The sprawling property was situated on a plot of lush green land bordered by trees and sloping slightly upward from old San Mateo Road (now Highway 92). While it was a hard farmer's life Frederico was experiencing, he was in America living in an idyllic rural setting suitable for raising crops and children. It would be seven long years before he was able to send for his beloved Maria.

It was not an easy journey for Maria. After spending a pounding month at sea traveling steerage and being processed through Ellis Island, she endured an additional two weeks traveling across country by train. The railway terminated in Oakland. From there she was to take the ferry to San Francisco, where it was agreed she and Frederico would meet at the Ferry Building at the foot of Market Street. And then he saw her. They rushed to embrace with a weary and bewildered Maria collapsing into his arms. But not before Frederico's eyes, darting to her bosom, saw a tag boldly marked, "Maria Puccinelli—San Francisco, California." Just like a parcel from heaven.

They were married in St. Peter and Paul's Cathedral, in San Francisco on March 31, 1918. It was Easter Sunday. Her somber wedding dress, though not distracting from her radiant face, was in stark contrast to the Easter finery milling around Washington Square. A spin around the Presidio in a horse-drawn carriage was considered *enough* of a honeymoon.

Maria's life in America then started when she traveled to her new home: the farm in Half Moon Bay. This entailed a ride by trolley to San Mateo. From there the stage (really an old bus) took them over the hill to Half Moon Bay. She didn't even mind all the cooking and laundry she must then do for the seventeen working hands on the farm, as long as she was with Frederico.

Within two years, the Giorgettis were able to purchase their own home: a summer cottage owned by a doctor from Sacramento.

The cottage was situated in a subdivision named the "Arleta Tract" southwest of the town proper, on the west side of the highway.

*   *   *

On a certain foggy, damp night, as befits this time of year on the Pacific coast, with just a smidgen of moon trying to break through the haze, if you just happened to be walking down a certain street in Half Moon Bay, you could hear the faint cries of someone in distress. While Maria is not normally wont to show her emotion (least of all to cry out in pain) this ordeal had been going on far too long—fifteen hours to be exact.

It was only three months ago that she went to the doctor. In spite of working in the fields along with Frederico, she was putting on weight and was not feeling her usual self. She was tired all the time. What a blessed surprise to hear the doctor say she was pregnant. Being a strong woman, she was able to endure the pain and the arduous journey this baby was taking coming into this world, but she did have to let out a much-needed groan or cry from time to time.

Since Maria did not speak English, she was fortunate in that the local midwife spoke Italian. They understood each other as the midwife silently went about nurturing Maria, comforting her. The midwife was adept at delivering babies—after all, she lived in town and was readily available—but this baby was becoming troublesome. It was up to her to bring this child out and bring it out she would. She spoke quietly and reassuringly, "Fatte pace, Cara Mia (be peaceful, dear one)." And as she caressed Maria's abdomen, another surge, "Tutto va bene (All will be fine)."

Maria thought, "God wouldn't bring me over here only to die giving birth."

It would be three more arduous hours before Leo Peter was born in the wee morning hours of December 11, 1920, weighing in at twelve and a half pounds. A beautiful and healthy baby, Leo was gently placed in his bed: *a padded wooden artichoke crate.* "Grazie, Dio," murmured a grateful midwife.

Three days later, the doctor arrived in town and pronounced Leo a healthy specimen. Unfortunately Maria would never bear another child.

Leo became the adored but disciplined only child of Maria and Frederico Giorgetti.

*   *   *

Since his mother did not speak English, Leo's early years were spent as if he lived in Italy. He repeated first grade because his mastery of the English language was insufficient to carry him to the next grade level. That didn't stop him. As a young child, he understood the family principle of working together so everyone could benefit. When not attending school, he worked in the fields picking artichokes and Brussels sprouts. He would shoot birds and send them to market with his father's harvest. Each bird would bring in 50 cents.

Creating ingenious ways to earn money was instilled in Leo at an early age. Since gophers were a constant nuisance in this farming community, one of his creative endeavors was to set gopher traps on the neighboring farms. Before going to school every morning he would check his many gopher traps and on lucky days the farmers were happy to pay the handsome fee of 10 cents per gopher.

All monies he brought home were put in the common pot. He observed, respected, and embraced the traditional Italian family values.

A.P. Gianini, founder of the Bank of America, would drop by the house to visit from time to time as he did to other neighbors and if Frederico needed help, A.P. would ask, "How much?" A.P. would stop by a few months later and Frederico would pay him the amount borrowed. They became friends.

It was an exciting day on Sundays when the peddler came by to sell household goods, clothing, shoes, and just about anything. Maria looked forward to the "pedelo" coming. She bartered for the items she needed, Maria speaking in broken English and the peddler trying his best Italian but spoken with a Yiddish accent. As bartering was the custom in Italy, the peddler understood it and naturally adjusted his price accordingly. They became friends and more often than not, the "pedelo" would stay for Sunday dinner. Leo also counted the days until he could see the dusty van approaching as the peddler always had a Hershey bar for him.

Sundays were special days at the Giorgettis' modest home; it was Maria's time to shine. Never knowing how many would attend, she would nonetheless start early to prepare her magnificent feast. Always soup would be served followed by antipasto. Then came the pasta. Frederico's private "Estate Bottled" wine and subsequently, maybe a delicious rabbit with polenta and sauce, accompanied all of this having been lovingly prepared on a wood—burning stove. Usually there were ten to fifteen guests and it was a marvelous time for Maria. Leo also benefited from this social interaction. Since he was an only child, and rather shy, at an early age he would run into the fields and hide when visitors arrived.

As the Sunday tradition continued, Leo blossomed into an outgoing child.

Indispensable to the Giorgettis' household were their animals, especially Dolly and Bill. These two fine specimens were the workhorses. This species of horse was smaller, more agile, and just as strong as the plow horse, which is exactly what Dolly and Bill did: Plow. Walking proudly and steadily in front of Frederico, they pulled a V-shaped iron plow, churning out the black loam, like waves, into precise furrows. When it was necessary to cultivate, only one horse would be required to pull the cultivator, with its steel blades reaching down to aerate the soil.

The rest of the menagerie consisted of two dogs, several cats (with no names as they were considered dispensable) barnyard chickens, rabbits, a couple of pigs, and Maria's pet canary, Stevie. These were all outside animals except Stevie who enjoyed a perch in a cage suspended in the back-porch off the kitchen. As Maria would sing her Italian ditties, she would look to Stevie and coo, "Canta, Canta (Sing, Sing)," and together they would sing and sing, soaring together as Maria cooked. One hot day as Maria was cooking her chicken cacciatore, she had left the back door ajar, and screeching interrupted their chorus. Looking around she saw one of the cats had sneaked in and was hanging from the cage with its claws reaching out for Stevie. Not wasting a minute—*whomp*—Maria swung around with the skillet, cacciatore and all, annihilating not only the cat but poor little Stevie as well. It was a sad day for Maria, but Leo soon bought her another canary, which she would soon sing to as well.

Big Dog Jack had the sole responsibility of barking if strangers approached and was known as the watchdog.

Buddie, a fox terrier, was the "ratter." Put him in the barn with the hay and he would root out the rats and mice.

The cats were kept around the premises to keep the gophers in check.

Once, when Leo was a little older, wild dogs threatened to get out of hand in Half Moon Bay. Fred Simmons, the constable, asked Leo and several other young boys to kill them, thus saving the slaughter of the area's farm animals. Leo mounted Dolly, along with his trusty rifle, and joined this posse of boys. Riding bareback, with only a hackamore (a bridle made of rope for guidance), he rode Dolly over the fields and down to the ocean at full gallop in pursuit of the outlaw dogs. Leo's rifle was a 22-gauge single shot bolt action, but it had a flaw: it wouldn't eject the shell after firing. So riding full-tilt over the land with an open pocketknife clasped between his teeth, he would have to grab the knife, deftly remove the spent shell from the casing, before replacing the knife between his teeth. He would then reach into his pocket, obtain a new shell and reload the rifle. Since the dogs were not only a menace to the farm animals but to the people, the boys felt a sense of accomplishment as they counted the tally: 14 dogs.

I should interject here some of the games Leo and his friends would play. In some cases both boys and girls would participate.

One game was called "Andy Over." Now I don't know Andy who, or over what, but this is how it was played. What you needed was a barn, a softball and six or eight boys. The boys were divided into two teams, three or four boys on each side of the barn. One boy would throw the ball over the barn and at the same time his team would yell "Andy Over" and they would run to the other side. The boy on the other side of the barn who caught the ball would hide it behind his back and wait for the other team to appear. Not knowing who had the ball, the ball-thrower and his team would be at the mercy of the boy who caught the ball as they ran into this hostile territory. A quickly thrown ball, aimed just right, would find its mark and eliminate one kid sending him to the other team. The object: obviously the team with the best eye for hitting the moving targets would accumulate all of the opposing team to their side and thus win the game.

Then there was the classic game of marbles, which necessitates all players to hunker down on the ground around a large circle drawn in the soil. Holding their colorful glass agates between forefinger and the knuckle of the thumb, a flick would send it speeding toward the opponent's marble, hopefully knocking it out of the circle.

The game of hide and seek is not new but in Half Moon Bay this was not your sissy-face normal hide and seek. No siree. These ten-and twelve-year-old boys would find themselves a girl partner and while the "seeker" was counting to one hundred, eyes closed, some "hiders" would head for the nearest haystack for a little snuggle time until found.

But many of the boys' games were more like practical jokes.

In fact, the town of Half Moon Bay, with just a population of 800 in the 1920s, was not ready for the antics that Leo and his friends would pull.

There existed in town, in the middle of Kelly Street just east of the intersection of Main, a 120-foot flagpole. One Halloween night, while hanging around with some older friends, and having escaped the single night watchman's vigilance, these mischief-makers not only managed to somehow disconnect an outhouse from its moorings but to raise it to the top of the aforementioned flagpole, not to be discovered until dawn's early light since no one happened to look up before then.

My favorite antic was called the "posthole game." Occasionally, young friends or relatives from San Francisco would spend time visiting Half Moon Bay. Usually this was in summer. Also, usually in summer, the local boys had chores to do and sometimes it was digging postholes for fences. Wanting to hang out with the local boys, it was not uncommon for some unsuspecting city boy to inquire about helping out. Well, sure. "Hey, Joey, I need some post holes. Go into Marsh and Cunha's Feed and Fuel on Main Street and get me some post holes," requested Leo.

Lickity split, Joey ran into town. "Leo Giorgetti needs some postholes," he blurted out.

"Darn," replied the burly man on duty, "I just sent the last batch away just a half-hour ago. Sorry, son, just tell Leo I should get some in by eleven o'clock tomorrow."

Wanting to continue to be helpful, the next morning Joey made another trip into Marsh and Cunha's and was told that the shipment got hung up and should be in later that day. It usually took two and sometimes three trips before Leo or his friends would crack up and the city boy knew he had been taken. He would guffaw right along with them and become a part of the conspiring group ready to send the next turkey for postholes.

Once, as a child of six, Leo took a friend into the cellar to show off his father's vintage wine. Naturally he turned the spigot and naturally wine came dribbling out. When little Leo tried to turn the spigot off, not naturally the wine kept flowing. Not knowing what to do and knowing instinctively he was in trouble, he did the only thing a six-year-old would think to do. He stooped down, put his mouth to the flow and proceeded to try to eradicate this monstrous debacle. He drank until he could drink no more! His friend than took over. This continued until two bodies barely resembling six-year-old boys were lying prone on the cellar floor as the spigot continued to drip the precious wine.

As luck would have it, they had neglected to close one half of the upward slanting cellar doors thereby leading to their salvation. But only temporarily I assure you. He had yet to face his father.

I don't think Leo ever outgrew his love for antics as you will see later!

During Leo's growing-up period, Maria was quietly saving her quarters and nickels and thinking about her progeny and their future.

*   *   *

Sometime after the turn-of-the-century a railroad was proposed for the coastline from San Francisco to Santa Cruz. It was appropriately named the Ocean Shore Railway. With such availability to the seashore, easy access to beach properties was envisioned, and once the properties were subdivided, a building boom was expected up and down the coast. Also envisioned by the local farmers was a way of transporting produce to market in San Francisco.

Hopeful investors, succumbing to "Buy in California" promotions, bought the land and then sat back and waited for their coastal properties to increase appreciably. After the devastating 1906 earthquake, some people did move farther down the coast. Tracks were laid and a railroad station built in Half Moon Bay. An article appeared in the *San Francisco Chronicle*, dated July 1, 1908, with accompanying picture, stating the Ocean Shore Railway was shy of completion by only 38 miles. To raise the needed money for its completion, bonds were being offered for sale to the public touting an interest return of 5.34%.

But the boom never occurred. The automobile had arrived and maybe the railroad wasn't needed. Eventually, though, the railroad was completed but it wasn't long before washouts to the north eventually destroyed it. So the lots remained subdivided and whether or not they owned them, the local farmers would cultivate and grow produce on the land. Without the railroad, it would still take Frederico an overnight trip by horse and wagon to take the produce to market in San Francisco.

After many years, the owners or descendents of these investment lots would arrive in Half Moon Bay to check out their "California Property" only to find it worth less possibly than what they paid for it.

For years Maria had put aside her nickels and quarters, thinking about her son's future, and now all the quarters and nickels she saved were needed. The owners of the investment lots were now coming around to sell. Although they were asking $50.00 per lot, Maria would whip out $25.00 in cash from her apron pocket and say, "I givva you $25.00." Most usually they would take it. Thus, over the years the wise Maria accumulated twenty or so lots, never selling those around her. She wanted to establish her own Italian "Corte di Giorgetti" where her progeny could live "en famille."

Such was Leo's early life in Half Moon Bay, loving, learning and laying the foundation for what was to follow.

Frederico farming in Half Moon Bay, 1916.

Maria and baby Leo, 1921.

A 1908 ad in the San Francisco Chronicle touts the railroad that was to come to Half Moon Bay.

The San Francisco Ferry Building, where
Maria and Frederico met.

The sleepy town of Half Moon Bay,
California, before rerouting of Highway 1.

(Photo courtesy of Old America)

Chapter Three

ONLY AT THE HORSE

Diva Callas

A short time after we opened, about 11 o'clock in the morning, Mayor Christopher called. Maria Callas was in town with her husband, Menneghini. Would Leo do him a favor? "I'm sending her over. Give her anything she wants and send me the bill," requested the mayor.

"Si seguramento (Yes, of course)!" replied Leo.

So at the appointed hour a black limousine slid up to the front and the driver emerged to open the door for diva Maria and her husband. She was striking and every bit a presence. Menneghini was rather slight. Leo greeted them at the door and upon entering the first thing she saw was the rather impressive salad bar. She asked, "What's that?" in Italian and Leo answered her right back in Italian and handed her a prawn to sample. She was fascinated and proceeded to hand out prawns to the customers standing by. "Wait a minute," said Leo, "why don't you go behind there (indicating the back of the salad bar) and pass them out?" Leo then took the large white chef's hat off Benny the Chef and put it on Maria's well-coiffed head. He had trepidations about this but he was caught up in the moment. Apparently Maria was too.

For a half hour, she served prawns, crab legs and other delectables to the customers and even those who shunned salad bars took advantage of the situation. Maria lived it to the hilt, making a show of it in grand style. All the while Leo, Menneghini, and all the customers were enjoying their own private performance.

Leo was certain they would go out of business if he continued this crab leg give-away any longer, so he gently guided Maria into the dining room. Leo chose Maurice, a French waiter just off the boat from France, for their host. Naturally Maurice seduced Maria with his charm as they conversed in French. Maria was having a marvelous time.

At one point Leo ventured over to the table to see how things were and she said, "sit, sit, sit!" Being an up-front kind of guy, Leo said, "Maria, I must say you do not seem the tempestuous diva I've heard about. You're friendly and good natured and I find you quite a lady."

Obviously flattered she responded, "You are very kind and I will never forget your hospitality." Then she added, "Forse sono tutti I due (Maybe I'm both)."

When it was time to leave, Leo and Maria exchanged hugs and double-cheek kisses.

Mayor Christopher heard about the fun and insisted Leo send him the bill. Leo did not.

Mystery Woman

A beautiful woman would come into The Horse regularly. Her black sleek hair, cut into a chic bob, just above the shoulder, would swing lazily if she turned her head. She did not wear the bouffant style that was popular at the time. Her clothes, softly tailored in understated colors, appeared molded to her figure. She always arrived alone. She always left alone. She was not one of the models who frequently visited.

Along came a regular customer named Herbie, a married man, who fancied himself quite the lady's man. He, on the other hand, would always arrive with one or two friends in tow. The time was always soon after 5:00 p.m.

On one particular evening, given Herbie's reputation and having previously noted the elegant woman's presence at the bar, his friends challenged him to make his move. His friends expected the usual—slouching or sitting next to her and giving the signal to the bartender for drinks. It was always good fun and he never struck out. This time, much to his chagrin and surprise, it was different.

After a couple of minutes, one could see the elegant lady's head shaking from side to side. Herbie had finally struck out. This was going to be hard to live down.

Soon after Herbie returned to his friends, the lady at the bar left.

I know why she shook her head. I know why she left. I know her name. Her name was Dan.

Mabel and the Cop

One beautiful morning, Leo opened the doors at 11:00 as usual when an apparition resembling Popeye's Olive Oil walked in and headed for the bar. She was a sight to behold, wearing a flimsy bathrobe with slippers on her feet and her stringy hair attempting to escape from a "snood" (a flimsy hair-net popular in the forties).

Leo approached her with trepidation. He cautiously greeted her and naturally asked her wishes. "I wanna drink," she said. When told the bar wasn't open yet, she launched into a tirade of profanity so vile it made Leo take a step backward. In her delivery of this litany and while calling Leo every name in the book, her robe was not doing the job it was designed to do and it was obvious to Leo and Pucci, the bartender, that she had nothing on underneath.

Leo thought, "Oh, oh, I'm in trouble." Always a fast thinker he reacted.

As Leo sprinted out the back, he yelled over his shoulder, "Hey, Pucci, keep an eye on her." So he was off to fetch Mike, the Irish cop (really) who walked the neighborhood beat. Luckily Mike was not far—only a block away. (How different San Francisco was then!) He told Mike about the woman and together they walked back to The Horse. As soon as they walked in the door, Mike stopped in his tracks.

"Ah, Mabel, whatta ye be doing down here? Ye know ye belong on the other side."

With a look of recognition, she said, "Ah, I'm sorry, Mike." Ever the gentleman, Mike took Mabel's arm and escorted her out the door. Whew!

I should explain that Mabel lived in a distressed area, which was, at that time, around Third and Mission, off Market a short walk away from The Horse. She had apparently wandered away and did so regularly from the sound of things.

Every city has one. San Francisco is no exception. During the 1950s until recent years, San Francisco's skid row centered at Third and Mission Street extending west. It takes a while but the inexorable march of neglect and abuse draws like a magnet those unfortunate souls who somewhere along their life's plan lose their way. As the souls gather, so do the profiteers who make a living off their misery. It's a compatible marriage until the segment of society, those who have attained some measure of success in life, or at least partly so, demand a part of that area to broaden and enrich their own lives, thus pushing farther back the boundaries of the degenerate.

It was in this environment that Mabel lived after gradually relinquishing the accoutrements and privileges she was used to until finally abandoning them altogether to live in her past dreams.

During the 1940s, not to anyone's surprise, two famous madams existed in San Francisco. To be a successful madam, it was necessary to have the right connections. Then life indeed was grand. The most well known was Sally Sanford who possessed a certain flair with her customers. You might say she had class.

It also doesn't hinder one's business to have the "juice" on a lot of important people. Sally also established legitimacy when she opened a restaurant and nightclub. She eventually became mayor of quaint neighboring Sausalito.

Lesser known was Mabel Malotte, who operated out of Pacific Heights. For some reason, while she curried favor and respectability from the establishment, it was denied her. She was who she was and made no pretense about it. Not trying to assimilate herself into a "legitimate" endeavor, she was constantly harassed by the powers that be.

Mabel's power and luck finally ran out and her doors closed for a last time. One can only wonder if she was the Mabel who wandered into The Horse on that day.

Spring on Maiden Lane

It came to pass that springtime, being a glorious time of the year heralding new beginnings, would be celebrated by the merchants of Maiden Lane. Each year at the beginning of spring, Maiden Lane came to life. Since the daffodil was the first spring blossom to emerge each year, the merchants along the lane used daffodils to adorn the fronts of their businesses. Thus, ablaze in daffodils, the lane became a pedestrian Mecca for spring lovers intent on enjoying life. If you lived in the city or happened to be visiting at this time of year, you would possibly be made aware of this festive event by the local advertising. Herb Caen's column stated simply, "Don't miss the 'daffydils' on Maiden Lane."

This annual event had been in existence for some time when Leo and Sam bought the Iron Horse and they were determined to perpetuate it. They did so with enthusiasm for many years. The spring ritual usually occurred around April 7th. Art Bell, the florist on Maiden Lane, and also the unofficial "Mayor of Maiden Lane," shipped five hundred thousand blooms for the occasion.

For two blocks down Maiden Lane it looked like flower land for one week. On one day during that week, each year, the city agreed to close the lane from noon to four o'clock to vehicular traffic. Pedestrians would stroll, the municipal band would play, and the festivities would include a celebrity Master of Ceremonies making sure everyone was having a good time. It was a beautiful and colorful event. Jerry Colona, Bill Cosby and Liberace were among those participating in "Spring on Maiden Lane," possibly because they were performing in San Francisco at the time. Ah, it was Heaven.

After the festivities, customarily the merchants and celebrity of the day would gather at The Horse for a late lunch to celebrate yet another rite to welcome spring.

On one occasion, at lunch, when Liberace was the celebrity, he became tired. It was exhausting carrying around the heavy finery he wore. He asked Leo for a place to escape, where he could find some quiet time away from people. Leo took him up to his mezzanine office and he was told to make himself at home. By this time the two secretaries were sitting there with their mouths agape. Liberace was in a talkative mood and forgetting momentarily his tiredness, he proceeded to regale his audience with unforgettable stories giving them memories they would never forget. After a while he left. Luckily for the secretaries that it was quitting time, since they were worthless at that point.

Sneaky Sammy

The following episode occurred and can effectively describe how to sneak into a busy bar or restaurant without being seen. I must warn you, it may be expensive and not necessarily cost-effective for your purpose.

Young, energetic Johnny Evans had just come into The Horse from his bartending job down the street. It was a change-of-pace for him, a little more action here, you might say.

In an already bustling atmosphere the doors burst open and much to the astonishment of Johnny and everybody else, two absolutely gorgeous, tall, black women strode in like they owned the place. All eyes were on their flawless, beautiful faces and exquisitely dressed bodies.

Since there was at the moment no place to sit, they stood around waiting, but only for a short time. Straight-up cocktails were served to them and they were so lovely the other patrons continued to gawk.

Meanwhile, back at the bar sitting on a lonely bar stool perusing the scene, Johnny sensed a presence next to him. As he held an olive poised, about to be eaten, Johnny turned abruptly. Much to his astonishment, there sat Sammy Davis, Jr. With this obvious sign of recognition and wanting to remain anonymous, Sammy raised his finger to his mouth—"shush."

Everyone's eyes remained locked on the gorgeous babes, and they remained locked until the lovely ladies of their interest were escorted into the dining room by the maitre d'.

By this time, with his back to the lounge area, no one noticed the newcomer at the bar who had sneaked in.

Only Johnny, who had trouble keeping his eyes averted, did.

We can only assume that the beautiful decoys had a very expensive dinner courtesy of Sammy Davis, Jr.

The Quiet Birdmen

On the last Friday night of each month a very interesting group of men would gather at The Horse arriving early and staying until all hours. The men all had something in common. They were pilots with some having distinguished themselves with acts of bravery or bravado breaking world records.

Charles Lindberg, himself a world record holder and distinguished pilot, in 1920 founded a society of like-minded individuals. The Secret Order of the Quiet Birdmen—QBs, as they would become known—spread across the continent and in the '50s I became their "hanger" in San Francisco.

Tony Quigley, a San Francisco attorney, known as "The Admiral" and himself a member, was responsible for bringing the QBs to The Horse.

As these QBs crossed the nation on business or pleasure they carried with them a book listing the locations of all the hangers with the understanding that they could drop in and be welcomed at any one of them.

Leo's son, Ricky, considered himself lucky when he was asked to "waiter" the QBs. He was fascinated as he listened to them relive their exploits, drinking, smoking cigars, and joking all the while. He thoroughly enjoying the camaraderie that exuded from this group. He was enthralled with their valor and looked forward to their meetings.

In later years, the group was comprised mostly of military and commercial pilots.

Lou Rawls

A singer from Chicago, Lou Rawls, visited me one night in the mid sixties, an unknown. Lou was a new guy in town entertaining at the Fairmont.

Like other celebrities who would gravitate to The Horse, so would Lou. He would come to San Francisco once a year for his gig at the Fairmont and he would always stop by. This went on for quite some time. Soon the world recognized Lou Rawls. But once a year, without fail, he still came to The Horse. Leo would reciprocate occasionally and take in his show at the Venetian Room on top of the hill.

As his tenure at the Fairmont stretched out, it was curious that with his new fame he would still be playing there. Leo ascertained that when Lou first came to San Francisco to sing at the Venetian Room, he signed a *twenty-year* contract to perform once a year for twelve days. As he gained stardom, fame and fortune, he continued to honor his obligation to the Fairmont. San Franciscans were honored to hear him. For the twenty years!

Spring on Maiden Lane.

Comedian Jerry Colona visits Spring on Maiden Lane.

Chapter Four

ENEMY ALIEN

On December 11, 1941, four days after the Japanese bombed Pearl Harbor and the United States entered World War II, Leo turned twenty-one. Since he was Maria and Frederico's only son and he wanted to enlist, he was able to persuade his mother to give her blessing only if he joined the Coast Guard. (During the war the Coast Guard was under the command of the Navy and Leo was considered a sailor). He would be close by, guarding the Pacific coast. So it came to be that he was stationed at Orick, California, situated on the northern coastline. During the war it was common, in fact it was often necessary, for service men to hitchhike across the country from base-camp to home when they were on liberty. Leo was no exception. His only means of travel was by standing on the shoulder of the lonely two-lane roads, and sticking his thumb out in the direction he wanted to go.

One bleak day, a weary traveler, he came home to Half Moon Bay, greeted his father and not seeing his mother asked, "Where's Mama?"

"Oh, she's on the other side of the highway. She can't come home."

"What do you mean, she can't come home?" So while a shocked Leo sat down, his father explained that soon after Leo left for duty, all local Italians who were not American citizens were considered "enemy aliens" and had to move to the east side of the highway (the present Main Street, that being the demarcation line).

So Maria lived on the east side of the highway and Frederico, who obtained his citizenship in 1929, remained on the west side tending to the animals and the farm. He would visit Maria every night. She was staying with a friend and was heartbroken. That is until Leo came home. This pip-squeak of a boot sailor with corn growing out of his ears rose up like Goliath and assured his mother he would take care of it. The situation was ridiculous. His mother, an enemy alien?

It must be noted here that there were purported sightings of lights flashing offshore or here and there an enemy sub sighted.

So Leo streaked out for San Francisco by thumb one day bent on ameliorating this situation.

Without hesitation or reservation and filled with righteous indignation, Leo entered the hierarchy of the Western Defense Command. General De Witt was the man to see. One by one this boot sailor laid waste the underlings, stating his case until he reached the fortress of a Colonel, and that was as far as he got. He figured, and rightly so, that he would not reach General De Witt. So Leo had better give this his best shot.

Obviously fortified with his "mission from God" demeanor, he respectfully explained the situation and ended his dissertation with, "I'll make a deal with you. I'm in the military. You have me. You know where I am. Let my mother go home and if she turns out to be an enemy, you can shoot me."

Within a matter of weeks, the order was rescinded and all undocumented Italians along the California coast were allowed to cross over the demarcation line to the west. In Half Moon Bay, in addition to Maria and Frederico being reunited, the baker, who lived on the other side of the demarcation line from his bakery, was able to return to work.

Maria's adulation of Leo grew, of course, since naturally, in her eyes, her beloved son was the one who wrought this miracle.

Maria and Frederico would face another obstacle in a few years that would again disrupt their peaceful lives.

Chapter Five

IN THE BEGINNING

Leo

L est you think Leo and Sam entered into this restaurant business devoid of any experience in the field, I can assure you that is not the case.

Leo and Sam met in the service during World War II. Both were in the Navy with Leo as Chief Petty Officer and head of the commissary. As such he ordered all food supplies, had a staff of 200 and was responsible for feeding 3,000 aboard the *S.S. Samuel Chase, APA 26*, known as "Lucky Chase" because it was never hit or damaged during its tenure in the African and Asian Theatres.

One heartwarming event stands out clearly during Leo's seagoing sojourn. It was toward the end of the war, late 1944, and the *Chase* was returning to San Francisco. As an amphibious troop landing carrier, it was carrying about 2,000 soldiers, marines and some sailors bound for home. For two years, the boys—and I mean boys, as they were twenty to twenty-two years old—had been on dry rations. Aboard the *Chase* the meals were adequate, but still powdered milk and powdered eggs would barely suffice. They had a tremendous desire for fresh milk: in fact, they craved it. As Chief Commissary Steward, Leo, being the "old man" at age twenty-four, had control of all the supplies on the ship. (Do you see what's coming?)

As the ship steamed closer to home an idea formed in Leo's brain and he decided to act on it. Through a radiogram to a contact in San Francisco, he was put in touch with Chris Katon, President of Spreckels Dairy located at Eighth and Bryant Streets in San Francisco.

"I have two to three thousand troops on board, heading for San Francisco. Is it possible to have enough fresh milk waiting for them?" asked Leo in the radiogram to Chris Katon.

This communication started when the ship was three hundred to four hundred miles out. A return radiogram continued, "Please call back with ETA and berth number."

In the meantime, Leo had checked in with the captain, concerned about how it would be paid for.

"Don't worry. We'll try it from this end first," the captain replied.

About fifty miles out another radiogram to Chris: "Arriving 10 a.m. tomorrow, Pier #9. Please acknowledge."

As the ship pushed ahead and pulled under the Golden Gate Bridge the troops were ecstatic just being home. Tears flowed as the ship passed under the bridge. Small flags appeared out of nowhere. Little did the troops know that another, sweeter homecoming was in store for them.

As the huge ship slowly maneuvered into place on the docks, Leo and the captain looked down from the captain's cabin. There below sat a gleaming semi truck clearly marked "Spreckels Dairy." It had worked. It was happening.

The captain grabbed the microphone and his words blared from the loudspeakers: "Attention, all hands obtain mess cups and prepare to receive fresh milk."

There was one micro-minute of extreme silence. Then chaos. As hooks were dropped over the side of the ship to pick up the five-gallon milk containers, the troops were running in all directions. Ladles were brought up from the mess, just in case.

A whole semi of milk, fresh from the dairies of Marin County was being unloaded in these containers all over the ship. Troops were waiting, cups in hand.

It took exactly two hours for all the milk to be slurped up by those kids. And, oh, by the way, the hero of the day was Chris Katon, who lost his only son in the war. No bill was ever received and Chris received letters from Congress highly applauding his action.

Sam

Sam was born in Easton, Pennsylvania, exactly six months before Leo was born, on June 21, 1920. As a young man he migrated to Fontana, in Southern California, to finish school before enrolling in the Coast Guard. It was at the Alameda Coast Guard Training Center that their paths crossed. Sam was a cook first class.

After the war, Leo went into the bakery business while Sam opened a chain of industrial cafeterias. It became quite a load for Sam and, wanting to expand, he asked Leo to join him. Their cafeterias soon were operating in 18 establishments: Sears, First National Bank of San Jose, Spreckles Sugar and four Bank of America branches including the main branch at 300 Montgomery Street, were some of them. The year was 1950.

It was at the 300 Montgomery Street site that "the boys" as they would become known (or those "Italian boys"), became acquainted with Carl Wente, the President of Bank of America.

It so happens that Carl's favorite restaurant, Solari's Grill, located on Maiden Lane, had recently closed. This was before the great days of an abundance of good restaurants and fine dining, and Leo and Sam took note of Solari's passing. Good restaurants and even great restaurants were in demand. In the blink of an eye they hatched a plan to acquire Solari's Grill. It really couldn't be called a deception, rather a means to an end. Now here's how they worked it:

Carl Wente would on occasion frequent the Bank of America Cafeteria if only for a cup of coffee. He got to know the boys and liked them.

The boys were becoming acquainted with Mr. Wente, biding their time, not knowing if or when something might happen but believing it would. When they saw Solari's Grill was available, it was time to pounce. After a "Good Morning" and "How are you boys?" they did just that. "Fine, Mr. Wente, can we talk to you a minute?"

They began. "Mr. Wente, ah, we found this property for lease not far from here and, ah, we have a very 'futuristic' idea. It's a good location and we'd like to open a restaurant."

Now Carl knew these boys were hard working and they seemed sincere. He had the foresight to judge them well. Without hesitation he said, "Let's go and see it."

Now Leo and Sam, knowing full well that Solari's Grill was a favorite haunt of Mr. Wente's, didn't let him know they knew. Mr. Wente was 6'3" and had hands like catcher's mitts. Now these hands were wrapped around each of the boy's shoulders as they walked up Montgomery Street, past Kearny, and when they turned the corner on Maiden Lane and faced the property, he exclaimed, "Oh, that's my favorite hangout!" In unison the boys responded, "Oh, really, well that's it. That's the place we're talking about."

The property appeared old and run down, and they stared taking it all in. Mr. Wente surmised that the boys were short funded and said, "I imagine you need some money," to which they responded, "You hit it right on the nose, Mr. Wente."

"How much do you think you'll need?"

Naively, and with hesitation, "Oh, about $20,000?"

"Come with me!"

With that short exchange they proceeded to walk back to the main branch of Bank of America. Mr. Wente took them downstairs where they encountered one of Mr. Wente's employees.

"Hey, Frank, take care of my two Italian boys here. Give them what they want and send the paperwork up to me."

With those beautiful words my financial future was at least launched if not assured.

Bob O'Dell, then owner of the Clift Hotel in San Francisco and Santa Barbara's, California Biltmore, owned the property at the time. A good lease was obtained and for three months Leo and Sam demolished the inside of the restaurant, including the use of a sledgehammer to destroy the brick ovens, then worked tirelessly to put it all back together in their haste to open. Their hard work paid off and while still maintaining their cafeterias, they were able to pay off their original loan from Bank of America in two years.

The iron horse hitches were out in front. A black bust of a horse graced the front façade. What would they name it? "The Iron Horse" of course!

And so I was born. My name and reputation were yet to be forged.

Chapter Six

FRIENDS

The Inner Circle

There is usually an Inner Circle of people, rather known as "friends of the owner" who would be granted certain privileges at almost any restaurant, with The Horse being no exception. Or they would be in attendance at various functions during "closed" hours. Inasmuch as there were two separate banquet rooms, many of these affairs were held there.

First it was Ed Farrah who visited to see his friend, Leo. Ed owned a clothing store in San Francisco with his father. Then Ed brought a friend, Joe Nucatola, who owned a San Francisco restaurant, Kerry's. Then it was natural for Joe's cousin, Teddy Amirro, to join the group for frequent visits. Another day, Joe's good friend, Howie Verfall, began to accompany him. Howie was called a "Ragman" as he was in the garment industry manufacturing business. So now we have the nucleus, the core, of the "Inner Circle of Friends of the Iron Horse."

Soon after, Augie Mariucci and Leo Koulos (referred to as Leo II) joined this princely group, all being young and single. We could include other regulars in this group, like Vince Tringali, but while they were regulars they might be married or otherwise unable to participate in the circle's all-for-fun antics. Their ages ranged from 21 to 34. Leo, divorced in 1956, was the eldest.

These friends bonded for better or for worse.

The following roster comprised this Inner Circle and helped create the pulsing, creative energy flowing from The Horse. Nobody was immune from their antics and sometimes pies would fly.

Joe—Tall, handsome, suave Sicilian, fun, s—disturber.

Augie—All heart, Mr. Good Guy.

Teddy—Joe's cousin. The Savior. Mr. Cool, lover boy.

Howie—A Jew. Another Mr. Cool, cries when laughing too hard, fun.

Leo II—A Greek. Defers to his senior, Leo I. Debonair, lovable, personality plus.

Vince—Another Sicilian, gregarious, volatile, competitor, Loyal.

Ed—A Lebanese. Mr. Suede Shoes, well dressed, debonair.

As these friends became involved with members of the opposite sex, then they too were included in the circle. Take, for instance, Jan.

Joe "movie star looks" Nucatola was at The Horse one evening, trolling, when good friend Howie (Mr. Cool) walked up with a darling red head. Seems Jan had arrived with a girl friend to have a drink. It was Howie she met and visited with. Since he was involved with someone else, he apparently did not want this one to get away. So, ever the Prince, Howie introduced Jan to his friend, Joe.

Jan had an infectious giggly personality and was instantly liked by everyone. One of her attributes was a "cute little butt." Because she was from the apple state of Washington, that particular part of her anatomy was henceforth referred to as "apple butt."

With everyone's approval, a courtship developed between Joe and Jan and she became a part of the Inner Circle putting up with the antics of this San Francisco Mafia.

In 1967, the first championship football game (which was in 1969 to be called the Super Bowl) was being held in Los Angeles at the coliseum. The Green Bay Packers were playing the Kansas City Chiefs. Pete Rozelle, then Commissioner of the NFL and AFL, had given tickets to Leo. So Leo, Joe and Jan decided to go.

While staying at a local hotel they ran into Frank Alioto, owner of the San Francisco's Alioto's Restaurant on Fisherman's Wharf. Frank, cousin of Mayor Joe Alioto, invited them to join him the following day for a ride to the coliseum. "Be out in front at 10:30," he said as he left.

The next day, as Jan would recall, three stretch limousines were waiting in front of the hotel. When she entered one she was surprised to see it full of men: Alioto's family from Milwaukee. In fact, all three limos were filled with black-suited men. It seems Jan was the only female in this entourage. As she squeezed in next to one of the men with Joe following close behind, feeling intimidated, and for the first time in her life non-talkative, she hunkered down and didn't say a word during the entire ride to the game.

When the limos arrived, did they disgorge the passengers in the front? No, they proceeded straight onto the field below their seats! Jan, in her lavender sweater dress with matching heels, and her new friends were ceremoniously greeted and escorted from their kingly carriages in front of the whole stadium. When the game was over, the process was reversed. The three loyal limos arrived at their feet to load their precious cargo. She would never forget that day.

Joe and Jan were married at The Horse. Jan is still a smashing red head. Joe has a full head of white hair.

Allison and Howie

The most enduring and endearing tale of the Inner Circle is the romantic story of Allison and Howie.

One day, Howie walked in with a bobbysoxer, an-honest-to-God bobbysoxer. She was a darling blond girl wearing a pleated skirt and saddle shoes. Now Howie was a strapping, handsome, eligible 40-year-old bachelor at that time and he was duly razzed.

Now in those days, special security forces were hired by the Police Department to frequent downtown establishments. So when our friendly neighborhood special security cop would come in from time to time, if Allison, the bobbysoxer was there, she would dash to the ladies restroom or discreetly cover her face so as not to be seen. One would think she was avoiding the police. She was, we found out later. This continued.

A couple of regulars, Joe and Howie, had February birthdays. So did Allison. It was time for a joint celebration. Just before the party, Allison, looking very sheepish, took Howie aside and said, "I'm sorry I didn't tell you sooner, but I'm not 21 yet." Howie, feeling good, and assuming she was 20, didn't care. He responded, "That's OK, we'll celebrate that next year."

February rolled around again and another party was planned. By this time, Howie and Allison were really getting serious. Howie wasn't at all put out and again assumed she was 20, when Allison again mentioned in passing that she wasn't yet 21. So, now we know the reason for Allison's subterfuge in the restaurant and her avoidance of the cop—she was only 19! She would stay in the restroom praying she wouldn't be arrested. She would be *so* embarrassed and what *would* her mother think?

The courtship blossomed and in the natural scheme of things pertaining to the heart, Howie and Allison got engaged. The date was set. They were to be married at The Swedenborgain on December 15, 1968, and the reception was to be held at The Horse. In the car on the way to get their marriage license, Allison leaned over to Howie, and with her hand coyly over her mouth repeated a familiar phrase, "Howie, I'm not yet 21, not until next year."

So, Allison had three birthdays celebrating her 21st birthday!

To further complicate this match made in heaven, dutiful daughter, Allison, sent a list of those participating in the wedding to her parents. Now her mother was a member of the D.A.R. (Daughters of the American Revolution) and her father was a Harvard business school graduate and curator of a museum. Allison had been raised in this upper-middle-class WASP family. So not only was she marrying a Jew, but when her mother saw the list of names: Joe Nucatola, Augie Mariucci, Leo Giorgetti, Teddy Amirro, she said, "You are NOT marrying into the Italian mafia!"

On the day of the wedding, continuing the cycle of pranks that this group seemed bent on pulling, Joe "heartthrob" Nucatola, dressed in his finery, not resembling a maintenance man, and feeling devilish, somehow found a broom, and knowing the bride's parents' arrival was imminent, proceeded to sweep off the steps of the church just as the bride's parents pulled up to the curb.

Allison and Howie were duly married and the reception was held here at The Horse.

Ed and Betty

You've heard of going to the ends of the earth to seek the identity of some fair damsel that you have just met, seen or heard about.

A certain member of the Inner Circle fulfilled his desire in a most unique way with the help of friends.

Naturally it happened at The Horse.

Howie Verfall and Ed Farrah had come into The Horse for lunch. For them this was rather routine but what happened that day changed Ed's life forever. As they approached the bar for a drink, Ed stopped dead in his tracks. Sitting just below the steps in the dining room was the most gorgeous girl he had ever laid eyes on. He must be dreaming. Of slender build with brunette hair and delicate features, she was having lunch with a girlfriend completely oblivious to the stirring of emotions in her nearby voyeur.

"Look at her, Howie, isn't she gorgeous?"

"She is that," replied an equally admiring Howie.

Now Ed had been coming around for sometime and beautiful girls were in and out regularly.

He started asking around and no one knew her.

When she arose to leave with her friend, Ed didn't know what to do. He grabbed Leo in desperation. "You have to help me—think!"

With Ed frantic as the girls walked out the door, Leo remembered that when she came in there was no table available so he took her name and wrote it down. "The wastebasket!" He exclaimed.

The two detectives took the wastebasket to a corner area where they emptied the contents scrap by scrap until: "Here it is!"

Her name was Betty and now all they had to do was find her.

San Francisco in the '60s was a small town. With all the contacts the Inner Circle had, it was only a matter of time before Betty's place of employment was found.

Ed was no slouch in pursuing her. He sent a note with flowers. When he received no reply, he sent her more flowers and then called her. She was polite but firm, "Sorry, but I just can't go out with you."

So he sent more flowers and another note. In fact he sent her flowers once a week. Eventually Ed's persistence paid off and she agreed to go out with him. So they dated and, like all fairy tale endings, they did fall in love and get married.

Only at the Horse!

Augie

Once in a while we are blessed with a soul put here on Earth to enrich our lives. Not in a religious or spiritual way but in a way that nonetheless lightens our load, makes us laugh, and by doing that helps ease our day-to-day travails. Augie Mariucci was just such a soul. At 5'5" with a girth that attested to his love of good food, he was a giant of a man bent on having a good time and bringing others along for the ride. His heart was as big as he was.

Augie was born in San Francisco, and grew up in San Francisco, in the Excelsior District. In this eclectic neighborhood he met Ed Farrah and they became lifelong friends. Always popular and fun to be with, at an early age Augie worked in the produce section of a grocery store on Chestnut Street, in the Marina District. Wanting something more than that in his life he gradually attained the knowledge and stature to deal in investments, primarily second mortgages. Everyone trusted Augie and he was a natural success: unpretentious, dependable and likable. It was into this milieu that he met the cast of the Inner Circle and, not yet married, became a member.

Augie seemed not too interested in finding the love of his life and settling down. He was having too much fun playing the field. One very special and unique thing he did caused many a heart to throb and, in some instances, to break. He returned from a trip to South America with a bag of uncut gemstones—smoky topaz.

He had a jeweler friend mount these stones. So now we have smoky topaz rings, with several of them being very impressive looking.

Now this is what he did with them: When he dated a lady he would give her one of these rings. The relationships were fleeting and the process repeated itself often. I sometimes wonder what would happen if all his dates came to The Horse on the same night and all wore their topaz rings. Well, we won't even contemplate that!

Many years later, when Joe saw a topaz ring on the finger of a friend's date, he jokingly commented, "Oh, you know Augie Mariucci." The comment didn't sit well with her date.

And then Augie Met the "Tall Girls"

San Francisco, being a city of conventions, one year hosted the "Tall Girls of America" convention. The criterion for attending, obviously, was to be at least 6' tall and to be a girl.

San Francisco opened its arms to these gorgeous gals and as they spread out over the city to enjoy the sights and sounds, it was inevitable that they crossed paths with our Augie. We can only imagine the dialogue that persuaded six of them to accompany this pied piper to The Horse one afternoon.

Walking abreast through the double doors of The Horse strode 5'5" Augie, elbows linked to three reed-slim creatures on either side.

Ever the gracious host and without feigning surprise at this sight, Leo spread his arms wide in welcome, bowed slightly and graciously escorted them to a table in the lounge. But Leo's nonchalance was not reflected in the other patrons. The "tableau" of this jolly man accompanied by six beautiful giant creatures caused conversation to cease.

Even more so when Augie pulled some cigars out of his breast pocket and proceeded to hand them out to all who wished to indulge.

Revelry soon reigned, as no one wanted to leave. So it was party time at The Horse all afternoon. This event is still remembered with awe.

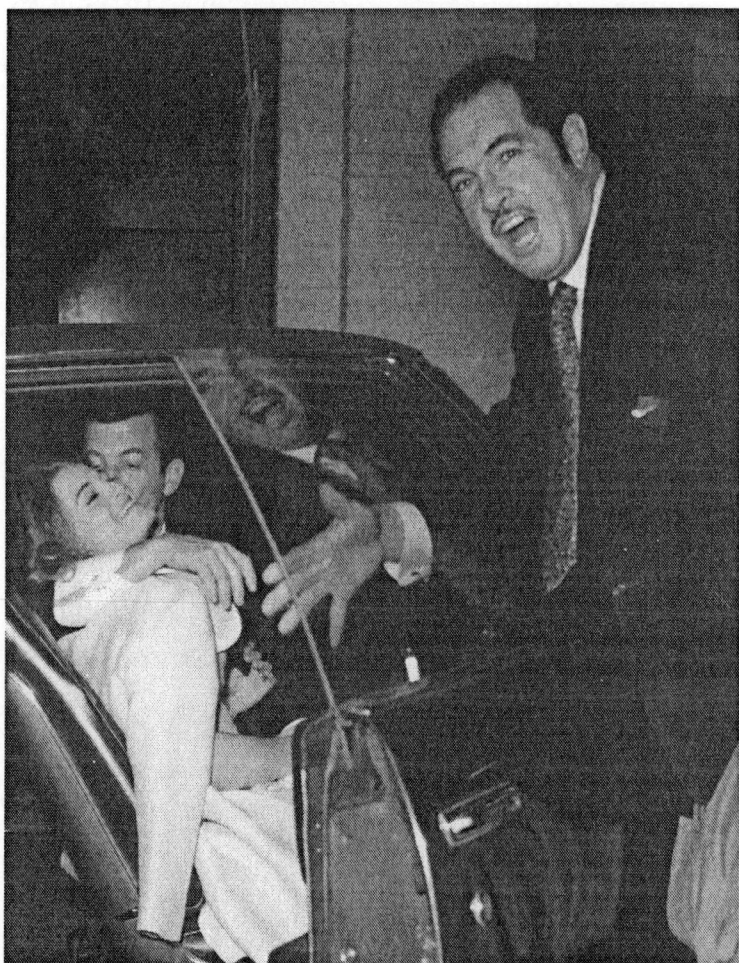

Just Married—Leo (r) clowns with Howie and Allison.

(Photo courtesy of Allison Verfall)

Chapter Seven

BACK IN HALF MOON BAY

Big Loaf

The war was over. Leo did not return to his farming life in Half Moon Bay. Married at the beginning of his service life, he chose instead to settle in San Francisco and raise a family.

He went to work at the Royal Baking Company on Mission Street and became a partner.

But even though he was working in the city, he was constantly thinking of his parents and ways to make their lives better. Because he loved to surprise his mother, one day, on a regular visit, he gave her one dozen flour sacks. She was elated. Maria took these cotton sacks, then bleached and hemmed them to make perfect dish towels. Eventually she made bloomers for herself out of these sacks: nice ones that billowed out slightly just above her knees.

Maria showed the towels to her neighbors and friends and soon Leo was gifting several of these friends with flour sacks.

But one day, Leo brought home some different sacks: colorful ones with "Big Loaf" imprinted on them. The company had changed the brand of flour it used. This caused a problem for Maria since "Big Loaf" would not bleach out. She pleaded with her son to bring the other ones, but they couldn't very well change flour again.

Nevertheless, Maria continued to use them not realizing that as she bent to her task in the fields, "Big Loaf" was emblazoned on her behind for the entire world to see.

Frederico's Fig Tree

The farming community of Half Moon Bay, situated on a sheltered plain along the mild California coastline, experiences ideal agricultural conditions. The black newly plowed fields are an invitation to romp and play in the soft earth and to enjoy sifting it through your fingers.

It is fertile ground for a myriad of floral species and at one time more daisies were shipped from Cozzolino's Nursery in Half Moon Bay than from anywhere else in the world. The rich soil welcomed the seeds of Brussels sprouts, beans, peas, corn, artichokes and pumpkins. The climatic conditions—too cold from coastal winds—were not suitable for growing tomatoes, citrus or fruit trees, however.

Now, every Italian wants a fig tree. By some coincidence and maybe by some miracle (possibly because Maria's two brothers, being priests, intervened), Frederico obtained a fig tree. He hovered over it, watching and nurturing it, until one year it produced a fig. *One fig*. The fig grew, ever turning its colors to become the deep purple-black fig it was destined to be.

The day arrived when Frederico could hardly contain his enthusiasm. He could almost taste its delicious, seedy contents.

He opened the back door to pick his prize only to see a "beca fico" (fig-eating bird) flying off the limb that held this fig. The bird had beaten Frederico to the kill. Frederico was devastated and vowed he would take revenge. He had propitiously planted the tree close to the house and the side door to the garage where he now placed a chair.

The next year, as the season grew near, the tree produced *two figs*. Frederico promised Leo, "No birds getta my figs."

As the figs repeated their cycle of growth, Frederico intensified his watch over the figs until the figs started turning their succulent inviting color. That's when Frederico took to his chair, his docile chicken on his lap, a cat stretched out at his feet—and watched for the bird. If one looked carefully, one would see a shotgun peeking out from the garage having been placed discreetly just inside the door. It was a 16 gauge. I might note here that it was, in the 1950s, against the law to shoot a firearm inside the city limits of Half Moon Bay.

The day came! A call came into the Iron Horse. Leo was called to the phone. He heard, "I gotta the bird! I gotta the "beca fico."

"You what?"

"I gotta the bird!" repeated an elated Frederico. "I gotta the sonofobitch!"

Meanwhile, back in Half Moon Bay, after the shotgun blast sounded through the neighborhood, a policeman drove up, as expected, and saw Frederico sitting in his chair with a chicken in his lap, enjoying the sun.

"Mr. Giorgetti, some neighbors reported hearing gunshots from this area. See anything?"

"No, I don't see nothing," Frederico replied. "I'm just sitting here with my chicken, smoking my pipe."

So the policeman left the scene of the purported crime without noticing the dead bird lying not 20 feet away.

Rest assured that Frederico's fig tree continued to grow and prosper producing many figs for the Giorgettis.

Chapter Eight

The 1950s

It's important to take the reader back in time, to the era, for an understanding of the need for—and ultimately why the success of—the Iron Horse.

The '50s arrived with a sense of enthusiasm. An anticipation and energy of beginning a new adventure, a chance to change what came before. We were dealing with Korea, that war having started in 1950, but we had survived the big one. Elvis Presley was singing and grinding to "Blue Suede Shoes" and "Heartbreak Hotel." You could buy a house for under $10,000. The colleges and universities were full of former servicemen taking advantage of the G.I. Bill to start a new life. It was a stimulating, prosperous, and lively time.

More people were feeling affluent. The fast-rising skyscrapers attested to the prosperity of the city of San Francisco and of the country at large.

The popular nightspots, "The Hungry I" and "The Purple Onion," were the ultimate vehicles for performers getting their start and were the jumping off point for Broadway and the entertainment world. The Kingston Trio, Jonathan Winters, Mort Sahl, Jose Feliciano, Carol Channing and Phyllis Diller were just a few of those performers who got their start in San Francisco. Young Johnny Mathis, a local boy just making his debut at the Blackhawk, a jazz club on Hyde Street, enjoyed coming to The Horse before his eminent fame took him elsewhere. It was at the "Hungry I" where Barbra Streisand appeared in the early stage of her career. She was signed to a six-week contract with a release clause. After two weeks, the owner Enrico Banducci let her go with the admonition, "Honey, you'll never make it here. You better go back to New York."

New inventions and expansions were happening all over America:

- Swanson Foods debuted its first frozen food
- Walt Disney unveiled Disneyland in July 1955
- In 1955, a jolly Santa Claus-looking-man named Colonel Saunders launched Kentucky Fried Chicken
- Also, in 1955, Ray Kroc changed forever the eating habits of America by taking McDonald's nationwide

On top of all this, we were mesmerized when our very own Grace Kelly became a princess in tiny Monaco in 1956.

A small square box had come to life, with its black and white figures, all over America. Those names and voices that we heard, and with whom we became familiar as we hunkered over our radios, became alive. We *saw* the Lone Ranger and Tonto. We *saw* Matt Dillon on "Gunsmoke." And soon that miniscule audience who owned a color television was rewarded with color.

It was a time of innocence, fun, and revelation. New life was springing up within us and all over America. We wanted to enjoy every minute of it.

There was a euphoric magnificent wellspring of confidence forming in the nation. We were back from the war and eager to re-start our lives. Entrepreneurship was rampant.

The celebrity restaurants were not yet in vogue. Not only were veterans and regular citizenry wanting to get on this prosperity wagon, first generations of European countries were coming to

America to make their mark. In the art world, abstract expressionism came into being and many of Europe's greatest in this milieu immigrated to America: de Kooning, Kline, and Reinhardt among them. The Bay Area had its share of entrepreneurs getting a foothold and never letting go of their dreams.

This was an exhilarating time at The Horse. Anybody frequenting The Horse would possibly see a visiting entertainment celebrity playing a local venue, or a sports celebrity in town playing at Candlestick Park. There were no Macy's, Mervyn's, or Nordstrom at that time. Union Square was a Mecca for shoppers. Narrow Maiden Lane was there, inviting shoppers to stroll down its delightful path. The large impressive stores situated around or within walking distance to the square were: White House, I. Magnin, J. Magnin, City of Paris, Gump's, Saks, Granite Bros, and Ransohoff. When couples would come to San Francisco from the surrounding area for the day, the wives would shop and meet their husbands afterward at The Horse.

In 1958, baseball's New York Giants moved west to San Francisco as the Brooklyn Dodgers moved to Los Angeles. So naturally, when the Dodgers played at Candlestick Park, they stayed at the Palace Hotel, which was situated nearby. The Horse became the gathering place for these athletes after play.

A typical evening after game time would find Don Drysdale or Sandy Koufax sitting on the steps leading up to the mezzanine with a slight path set aside for the cocktail waitresses bravely bearing their load. At these times the lounge area would be so jam-packed it was necessary to open the service bar adjacent to the kitchen in order to satisfy the thirsty throng.

In fact, one particular barstool on the curve of the bar as you entered The Horse was the unofficial perch for Johnny Unitas, of the Baltimore Colts, during football season, and for Stan Musial, of the St. Louis Cardinals, during baseball season. From that vantage point they could check out all the action. No names were placed on the seats. If they were occupied, Johnny and Stan would simply wait.

So the likes of Pee Wee Reese, Stan Musial, Pete Rozelle, Johnny Unitas, Sandy Koufax, Pete Rose and most other National League sports figures were seen at The Horse.

The Iron Horse offered a "window into the soul of the country at that time."* It was the era.

---

*Stephen Ives—A quote offered about his documentary *Seabiscuit* but apropos for The Horse.

Chapter Nine

BUSINESS AS USUAL

Pelican Stew

During the 1950s, 1960s, and 1970s more business was conducted around the white-clothed luncheon tables at restaurants than in the boardrooms across the nation. It was called the three-martini lunch.

There existed during this time, a prominent construction firm in San Francisco called Barrett Construction Co.

The city was enjoying a building splurge and Barrett Construction was responsible for, among many other projects, building the Third Street drawbridge near the present Pac Bell Stadium and the drawbridge at the end of Army Street. Beautiful St. Catherine Church in Burlingame, farther south on the peninsula, was also one of their projects.

Its President, John Jr., his brother, Dick, and the controller, George, were regulars at The Horse. They would come in every day of the week except Friday when they would meet at Tarantino's on the wharf, where, being good Catholics, fish was the entrée of choice.

If their secretaries or clients needed them, they could always be reached at either the Iron Horse or Tarantino's.

Norm Burke told the following story of the "Pelican Stew" to all who would listen.

While these executives came in almost every day, at a certain time each year, during crab season, Pucci the bartender would whip up a marvelous crab cioppino and the whole staff—which at that time consisted of approximately twenty men—would gather at The Horse for a feast and camaraderie. It was a tradition and something the men looked forward to each year.

One year, for some reason, the wives felt left out and wanted to be included in the dinner.

It soon became a problem for the men. They decided they would take the path of least resistance: they relented. But, it had to be a one time only affair devised so that the wives would not want to return. But how?

Taking Pucci (by name Mario Puccinelli and a cousin of Leo's) into their confidence—and a good thing they did too—they came up with a foolproof plan. Everything went superbly. Forty guests arrived on the ordained night with the wives getting their due recognition and making a grand procession up the stairway to the banquet room on the mezzanine. After drinks, Pucci brought forth his masterpiece.

The wives did not mention returning the following year. It seems Pucci had loaded the cioppino with more than enough garlic and pepper and for three days after the feast the worst possible taste existed in the mouths of the wives, like a dead pelican.

So thereafter it was called "Pelican Stew" and the men resumed their "men only" yearly feast of pelican stew.

Hoffa at the Horse

During the '50s and '60s San Francisco was considered a 100% union town. All the waiters, bartenders, waitresses, drivers and help at The Horse belonged to the union.

After Teamsters President, Dave Beck, went to prison as a result of a Senate probe revealed income tax fraud and theft, the AFL (American Federation of Labor)—CIO (Congress of Independent

Organizations) booted out the AFL. The successor to Beck was Jimmy Hoffa, former American Federation of Labor organizer. So, after Beck went to prison, Hoffa became the most powerful man in the union.

The local AFL Labor Council consisted of many different types of councils: i.e., canners, drivers, waiters, bartenders etc., all headed by Hoffa.

The councils would meet periodically in key West Coast cities: Los Angeles, San Francisco and Seattle. As leader of this great body, Hoffa would join the heads of these various councils at all of the meetings. These meetings were held to make sure that all the spokes of the wheel were kept oiled and operated smoothly.

Yes, you probably guessed. Since San Francisco was a prime West Coast headquarters, when Hoffa was in town, all meetings were held at The Horse.

I usually knew a meeting was imminent as the out-of-towners would arrive early and drop in the night before, usually hovering around the bar and sometimes staying for dinner.

The next day, it was usually lunchtime when they met. Fifty to sixty men, all dressed in dark suits and some wearing hats, would arrive and would head up to the banquet room. It was an all-afternoon affair with many hanging around into the evening.

I didn't suffer from this notoriety. As I said, it was just my calling to cater to the rich, poor, famous and notorious.

The Mighty Mustang

The call came through at 11:00 a.m. one day in the spring of 1965. The vice president in charge of operations of the Ford Motor Company would like to speak to Leo.

A special event was to occur on the West Coast and would The Horse be available to host a banquet in San Francisco? Simultaneous events were to be held in Los Angeles and Seattle.

Plans slowly unfolded with the event scheduled to take place in June. There would be local Ford dealers and national executives of the Ford Motor Company attending, maybe close to a hundred.

Lee Iacocca, the President of Ford Motor Company, would preside over the event.

The day arrived and at three locations on the West Coast the newest creation of the company would make its debut: the mighty Mustang.

At The Horse in particular the event started early in the day when the Ford Motor Company parked a younger and more colorful likeness of me on the street right under my proud countenance (not a nice thing to do but, hey, I'm here all the time, and besides I'm not the boss). It remained there, its shiny red paint glistening, for all to see, and I suppose it was a good thing for The Horse, since people were flocking in and out of my doors all day.

Early in the evening about sixty-five suited and important-looking men, including Iacocca, entered my doors and proceeded up the stairway to the banquet room. It was here that they toasted each other with the success of the newest member of the herd.

They were right to celebrate as the mighty Mustang has attained even greater popularity in the decades since it was launched. But the '65—especially a red '65—is still *the* most collectible.

Chapter Ten

TROUBLE ON MYRTLE STREET

L ife was peaceful and Maria and Frederico were prospering in the 1950s. After all, their son had opened a fancy restaurant in San Francisco. Maria was an American citizen now. Over the years she had acquired the modern conveniences. Although they were blessed with inside plumbing from the beginning, it was not until the early '50s that she experienced the pleasure of a remodeled kitchen with a gas stove and a new refrigerator. She was enthralled with television and she was seeing things she had never seen before. Life was indeed good.

That is until the notice came, followed by a frantic call to Leo at The Horse.

"They gonna move my house."

"Wait, Papa, who's going to move your house?"

"The government, they gonna move my house."

When Leo read the notice he wasn't surprised.

As the country was prospering again and new buildings were rising, new roads, highways and freeways were being upgraded and re-routed. America was on the move and massive freeways were under construction. Half Moon Bay was re-routing the highway that ran right through the middle of town one third of a mile to the west cutting through the Arleta Tract and right through the only lonely house that stood in its way.

"Why don't they go around, looka all the land?" an indignant and distraught Frederico asked.

With a patience born over many years of having to explain the sometime eccentric ways of America, Leo explained the necessity of having to build this new highway in a straight line, and thereby re-routing the heavy through-traffic away from town, which would indeed necessitate moving the house 150 feet to the east.

When the day came six months later, after all the red-tape had been settled, they were powerless to stop this infringement and docilely watched their home being carted 150 feet away thereby rendering their once peaceful home, surrounded by fields, a short distance from what was to become a busy thoroughfare.

Left behind was the cellar where six-year old Leo and his friend had drunk the wine from the wine barrel. Frederico not only made wine there, but it was also the primary storage for food staples and cured meat.

Since the new highway ran right through the property, not only were the precious fig tree and the garden demolished, but Maria's outdoor brick oven, the source of her crusty Italian bread, was also destroyed.

This was a terrible adjustment they made but adjust they did and soon their warm vibrant Italian life returned in full measure.

Chapter Eleven

CULINARY DELIGHTS

Since this story is about a restaurant, let's not forget the culinary part of me, the muscle and fiber, without which *I* would not exist.

Benny was our chief pantry man. He was responsible for all the glorious, famous salads that I was known for. His station was the main feature at the entrance to the dining room where patrons passing by could observe the awesome display of salads. As one would gaze over a handsome wooden bar to watch Benny work, his tall chef's hat perched on his head, his hands moving with lightning speed, it was impossible not to feel a sense of fascination and wonderment when one thought about the arduous path that led him here. A Filipino, he had survived the Japanese invasion of his country and served as aide de camp to General Douglas MacArthur during World War II.

But the wounds from the war had not yet healed. Noticing Benny's agitation whenever a Japanese person entered The Horse, Leo would somehow find something significantly useful to say engaging him in calming conversation.

Benny's assistant, Monaco Paule, equally dexterous in preparing dishes, had an interesting story of survival as well, which at the time was still painfully raw.

He was a scout in the Philippine Army when he was captured. After many days, forced by the Japanese to march to prison camp in the notorious Bataan Death March, he had just about given up but his feet kept going. The marchers were slowly trudging along a trail no bigger than a cow-path with hip-high grass growing alongside.

A few yards away, and in the distance, Filipinas, wearing long billowy skirts and straw cone-shaped hats could be seen toiling in the fields. Some were close enough to make eye contact—and that is just what one Filipina did with Monaco.

With a furtive look down, she wiggled her fingers and slightly moved her skirt. Monaco instantly darted down, made his way quietly and rapidly through the grass. As he reached her, she quickly raised her skirt and he darted underneath. He remained there, completely covered, for the length of time the Filipina deemed safe.

Thus, as one of the survivors of this infamous march, Monaco lived to bring his culinary skills to the Iron Horse.

Speaking of culinary skills, I should mention that our menu was exquisite continental fare—a combination of Italian mingled with French. At that time, veal was the meat de jour with dishes like Veal Scaloppini Sec, Breaded Veal Cutlet, Veal Chop, Veal Picatta, Veal Parmigana and Osso Bucco.

Veal Scaloppini was served with sliced mushrooms and a wine sauce.

Veal Picatta used capers.

Veal Parmigana was breaded veal with cheese and sauce.

Veal Scaloppini Sec consisted of veal sautéed with perhaps a light Marsala sauce and button mushrooms.

Osso Bucco was braised veal shanks with vegetable sauce served over risotto.

Medallions of beef was also popular as was Chicken Sauté Sec, Chicken Jerusalem, Chicken Cacciatore, Chicken Al Mattone, (fried in a skillet using fresh garlic with a specially-made stone placed on top of the chicken) and always marvelous French sauces. A cart was placed next to the table for mixing and serving salad. Blazing with a flambé was at its zenith and very popular with the patrons. Because of the three descending steps to the dining room, the carts were left on the lower level. Not only were they used for salads and entrées, but also Cherries Jubilee frequently was the night's romantic final course.

There was one vegetable that is not understood and therefore by being neglected deprives the uninitiated a whole world of savory ecstasy. It was the lowly artichoke.

Being from Half Moon Bay and having grown up, not only picking but also eating artichokes, Leo had his pulse on that market. The popular method was to boil the artichoke and serve it with melted butter if it was hot or with mayonnaise if it was cold.

How about tiny artichokes deep fat fried plain or enveloped in an egg batter? Also, the small artichokes are delicious cut in half, par-boiled and marinated in oil, vinegar, garlic and seasoning. Printed boldly on the menu was "Mama Giorgetti's Artichoke Frittata" which was a favorite:

eggs
mild Italian sausage
artichokes (fresh quartered)
chopped onion
salt and pepper to taste

But the piece de resistance was the No. 16 artichoke (so named because only 16 came in a box). Each one was trimmed, boiled and individually placed on a silver dish, one large artichoke per dish, surrounded by garnish including jicama spears and accompanied by a delicious dipping sauce:

mayonnaise
dijon mustard
lemon
worcestershire sauce
salt and pepper to taste

The waiters, splendidly attired in red cropped jackets over black pants, were instructed to carry this trophy in the palm of the hand with the arm held high. Making their way through the crowd with "excuse me, please," this masterpiece being carried through the dining room naturally caused people to exclaim in wonder, "What's that?" or "Wow," or "Look at that."

Presentation! Presentation! Presentation!
So take another look at your next artichoke.

Chapter Twelve

HORSE PLAY

Louie Louie

And so, it seems that the Inner Circle, having nothing better to do, continued to play practical jokes on each other. No one was immune. Not even the help.

An indispensable member of the Iron Horse help was a Chinese bus boy named Louie. He was well liked, worked hard and had a cheerful presence. The regulars called him Louie Louie affectionately. At the end of the cocktail hour and just before the dinner rush he would take up a broom and long-handled dust pan and proceed to sweep up the bar lounge area.

One particular evening a few Inner Circle regulars—Augie, Howie, Joe, Vince and Leo II—were sitting in the lounge in their favorite large booth near the salad bar. As Leo II observed Louie Louie engrossed in his usual afternoon chore, an idea formed. Leo II decided to play a little trick on him. He tore a $20 bill in half, folded one half so the 20 would show and shoved it with his foot as close to the salad bar as he could.

As Louie Louie was sweeping his way from the bar, he suddenly spotted the $20 and began to close in on it, sweeping here and there, but never taking his eyes off the bill. As the culprits were convulsing in their booth trying to suppress their laughter watching this dance, Louie Louie swept the bill into the dustpan and quickly disappeared into the kitchen. Two minutes later Louie Louie reappeared and coolly began to sweep around the tables and chairs, obviously looking for the other half of the bill. Finally, Leo II could not stand it anymore so he called Louie Louie over and told him he had lost half of a $20 bill somewhere and that if Louie Louie could find the other half he would split it with him.

Louie Louie than began a serious search of the entire dining room, moving chairs and continuing the sweeping looking for the elusive half bill. Finally, after about ten minutes, he ran off to the kitchen, magically appearing shortly thereafter with the bill clutched tightly in his hand and yelling, "I found it, I found it!"

Good to his word, Leo II gave Louie Louie $10 and thanked him profusely. The culprits had had their fun for the day and Louie Louie was none the wiser for the part he played in giving them this enjoyment.

As was his custom each day after his shift, he would say to Leo, "Mr. Leo, can I have a beer?" And continuing the pattern, Louie Louie would go to Pucci at the bar and with a confidence born of habit order a beer.

And the pulse goes on!

Louie stayed at The Horse for about ten years. Everybody loved him and his dedication and industriousness enabled him to send four of his six children to college.

Fire! Fire!

Oh, there he goes again. As flames erupt from the flambé cart, Leo is seen placing a fire extinguisher surreptitiously down by the feet of the Maitre d', Caesar.

Leo was not above enticing someone away from his or her current employer once he established that person could be an asset to The Horse.

That is exactly what happened with Al Martinez. During a sojourn to Palm Springs, and while dining at the popular "Flame"

Restaurant and nightspot, Leo observed a dashing figure. As Maitre d' of this elegant establishment, Al resembled the then popular and flamboyant film star, Caesar Romero. Leo decided then and there that The Horse had to have him. So Al Martinez, nicknamed "Caesar" became a colorful and permanent figure at The Horse, charming all those who entered my doors.

On those occasions when the flambé cart was used, Caesar was at his usual best. Not to be outdone and like a dance *a deux*, Leo would seize the moment to share the stage with Caesar.

During the preparation of the steak medallions, veal scaloppini, or flambé desserts, Leo would quietly place the bright red fire extinguisher on the floor by Caesar's feet and, much to the amazement of the diners, remark, "Can't be too careful!"

Al loved this charade and every time it happened he would laugh heartedly and carry on. The customers naturally were wide-eyed, wondering if this was really a concern. Al just smiled and said, "Not to worry, crazy Leo is just having his fun."

The regulars were used to this antic, as it was part of being at The Horse. The newcomers sensed the fun and energy and enjoyed it immensely. They would return.

Dr. Bob and the Model

In San Francisco, there was a popular dentist named Bob who had a clientele of, I guess, the World. Everybody loved him so he must have been noteworthy. However, he had one major flaw, which would backfire when he least expected it.

He was a jokester with a habit of doing "funny" things to the teeth of his clients. Mind you he chose them well, though. His criteria for choosing a victim: They had to have a sense of humor and be able to take a joke.

Now, it was not unusual in The Horse to see beautiful models strolling in and out on a daily basis. They worked at the top-of-the line stores of Union Square like Magnins and Saks, or at one of the three model agencies that was close by. One of the models was Pat M. And Pat M. was one of Dr. Bob's many customers.

On one noteworthy day Dr. Bob sent Pat M. out his office with a *black* tooth. Previously he had made a complete set of teeth for her so it was no trouble for her to remove the loathsome mark by removing her teeth. It is incumbent upon me to mention to the reader that I have no idea *why* Dr. Bob removed her teeth, but it *was* done.

Dr. Bob was a regular for lunch and he would always sit in a booth between the men's and lady's restrooms so he could watch all the pretty ladies go by on their way to powder their nose.

One fine day, Dr. Bob was here as usual, but he wasn't intent on watching the female sex this particular day as he was hosting a group of out-of-town dentists who were in the city attending a convention. I'll tell you, all was very serious at that table.

Pat had for some time been waiting for the right time to get back at Dr. Bob for the black tooth, and she quickly sized up the situation as *that moment*. Without any fanfare, Pat strode up to the table, took out her teeth and slapped them down right in front of Dr. Bob. To his horror and with shock registering on his face, and those of his colleagues, she said, "Here, take your goddamned teeth. They aren't worth shit." With that, she turned and walked into the restroom before Dr. Bob could say anything even if he was capable of it. He certainly couldn't follow her.

Now I ask you: How did Pat get her teeth back?

Caen Fun

If I may take a moment now to introduce you to someone who single-handedly brought more VIP's to The Horse than anybody, some very distinguished guests who spread my name farther across the globe: His name was Ken Macker.

He was not famous as you recognize "famous," but in his milieu he was powerful and very respected. He was a public relations man personified. Pete Rozelle was and is still famous. Ken Macker was Pete Rozelle's boss. With Philippine Airlines as one of his clients, Ken was instrumental in bringing the Vice President of the Philippines through my door. The Vice Mayor of Melbourne,

Australia, Sir Morris Nathan, was his friend and a visitor to The Horse many times.

Although Ken was unpretentious and unknown, his presence brought class to the establishment. But he was human.

One afternoon at The Horse in the company of Herb Caen, things must have been a little dull. So they decided to play a trick on Sam Marconi, the serious partner of the Iron Horse. They brought Sam Cohen, owner of a neighboring eatery into the picture. Herb had to line up their cast of characters perfectly to make this work. He alerted not only Leo, who was working the upstairs that day, but also their waiter.

The curtain was about to go up as Caen and Macker entered their favorite booth.

Naturally they ordered and were served drinks, maybe two rounds, but after that it appeared to Sam they were left alone. (If their waiter appeared they would shoo him away.)

Sam, working the main dining room, seemed puzzled at not seeing them served. As he approached their table, Herb bellowed, "God dammit, Sam, what do yah have to do to get service here?"

Sam apologized and looked around for their waiter who again approached and was summarily sent away as soon as Sam strode off.

At that moment Ken took the phone (always available), plugged it in the jack in the booth and called Sam Cohen. "Get your ass down here, we're ready," ordered Ken.

Very Shortly, I mean shortly, because the food was already prepared, what happened then caused customers to stare and Sam Marconi to almost bust a gut.

Through the back door strode Sam Cohen, apron on, towel draped over his shoulder, carrying a tray of food from *his* restaurant and a folding table on which to place it, next to the table where the entire world could see. Bringing food *into* The Horse?

When Sam observed this there was only one word that could describe him: apoplectic. Then they started laughing and he knew he had been taken. He turned on his heels and muttering obscenities, he stalked away.

Honestly, how can you possibly get mad at Herb Caen?

Chapter Thirteen

THE 1960s

With John F. Kennedy's slogan "to move the country forward again," he pulled an upset win over Vice President Richard Nixon in 1960. He inspired the throng gathered at his 1961 inaugural, a new generation of Americans, with his vision of a "New Frontier." The young of the nation were thrown the gauntlet, "ask not what your country can do for you, ask what you can do for your country."

In spite of the crises gripping the world (the Bay of Pigs fiasco, the division of Berlin into East and West, a Cold War looming), life was good. Change was definitely in the air.

When we entered the Vietnam War in 1965, a quiet revolution occurred. We wanted peace and love, not war. We could live in communes in peace and above all else, in love. Flower Children bloomed all over. Haight-Asbury in San Francisco, as the most popular gathering spot in the nation, was awash in unwashed bodies sitting on curbs singing and playing guitars. Psychedelic windows stared out at the passerby promising something close to nirvana. New folk songs were born and those singing them became idols: Peter, Paul and Mary, Joan Baez, Bob Dylan, and Simon and Garfunkle gave us a sense of peace and well being as we held hands and swayed to the music as we sang. "Puff the Magic Dragon" was a song on everybody's lips as was "Sounds of Silence" and "The Times They are a Changin'."

The Republican Convention of '64 held in San Francisco pitted a conservative Barry Goldwater against liberal Nelson Rockefeller. Goldwater was selected to try to defeat President Johnson who had been thrust into the presidency with the assassination of the popular Kennedy in 1963.

After 10,000 demonstrators descended on the Democratic Party's National Convention in Chicago in 1968, a frightened electorate voted Richard Nixon to the presidency.

We understood their decision but missed our friends in Canada riding out the Vietnam War. In San Francisco, vibrant life still existed. Popular dining spots were the Blue Fox, Ernie's, Doro's, Fleur de Lys, Bimbos 365, Enricos, Paolis and Tadich's. And the energizing pulse still permeated The Horse.

The suburban malls started their creep outward extending suburbia but not yet greatly impacting downtown business.

Candlestick Park hosted the 1962 World Series with the San Francisco Giants vs. the New York Yankees. Willie McCovey was at bat in the ninth inning with two men on, the score 4-3 Yankees, when Yankees' second baseman Bobby Richardson jumped high in the air and caught what would have been a home run denying the Giants the series. Ironically, Richardson was a San Francisco boy.

The Dodgers' Sandy Koufax retired in 1962 after a 27-win season.

Saks on Union Square was selling linen dresses for $19.95.

Playing at the Venetian Room at the Fairmont Hotel on Nob Hill, Tony Bennett touched hearts with his hit song, "I Left My Heart In San Francisco," on January 28, 1967.

We were a small town, a friendly town, a magnificent town, and a magical town. Times were good! Life was indeed good!

Amongst this euphoria, the Iron Horse beckoned those who wanted respite and those who sought its pulsing energy.

Who would guess that a horse could play host to the world?

Chapter Fourteen

SPORTS ILLUSTRATED

Heroes All

I had my fair share of young "wanna be" wives of the sports figures who hung out here. These regular habitués naturally became a magnet for the upwardly mobile, young executive or the masculine species in general and if meeting the sport figure Maggie Sue dreamed about didn't materialize, there was Mr. Mortgage Broker there with whom to share a drink and possibly dinner.

I do not know how many of these encounters turned serious but I do know that Leo planned and arranged for many engagement parties, weddings and receptions.

One day, Leo's teenage son, Ricky, was on the mezzanine doing his homework when Joe DiMaggio arrived to get a bite to eat. Noticing Ricky he asked Leo, "Who's that kid?" When Leo told him, "That's my son," Joe approached this wide-eyed kid and said, "Would you like to join me for lunch?"

Ricky just nodded.

He soon retrieved his tongue however as Joe started asking questions.

"Where do you go to school?"

He found out that Ricky played little league, football, and went duck hunting with his dad. Funny thing, though, although Joe rarely talked about himself, he started regaling Ricky with stories of his time with the minor league San Francisco Seals, and his advancement to and adventures with the New York Yankees.

After about an hour, Joe stood up, shook Ricky's hand and left. I think you could say that Ricky was dumbstruck. He did, though, finally gather himself together and went off to find his dad to share this memorable moment.

It proved an inspirational time for Ricky and served him well in his own experiences and success in life.

*   *   *

Both of Leo's sons, Rick and Bobby, attended San Francisco's St. Ignatius High School, which at that time was a private all-boys school. Since both boys played football, Vince Tringali, the coach then and highly regarded in San Francisco, became an integral part of the Giorgettis' life and thereafter a rather permanent fixture at The Horse.

At the end of the season the entire St. Ignatius football team would be hosted to dinner in the banquet room of The Horse. At one particular dinner it seemed that three Monsignors were loitering around the front door waiting for the event to begin. If this continued, black-garbed priests at my door, maybe a different interpretation of dining and evening fun would be cast upon this fine establishment. This could never happen. Leo could not stand it any longer. He went outside and politely invited them to come upstairs for a cocktail as they were "possibly" giving The Horse a different reputation.

Because U.S.C. head coach John McKay and assistant coach Marvin Goux scouted St. Ignatius, through Vince Tringali, they also became regulars at The Horse. In Marvin Goux's own words, "As soon as I knew I was flying to San Francisco, I would call Leo and place an order for Mama Giorgetti's Artichoke Frittata."

O.J.

One early evening in 1967, regular Ole Vince walked in accompanied by a very young handsome black man and an equally young black woman. Leo greeted them and seated them at a rather private table. Leo then sat down also as if he knew this young couple. They talked for a while and then Leo got up and left. Something important was happening. I knew it.

Here is what happened as told by Vince Tringali:

O.J. Simpson had become a legend in his own right, for good and bad. U.S.C. was recruiting O.J. and Marv Goux was the head recruiter for Northern California. He called me up one day and said Cal was doing some undermining stuff to recruit O.J. to play at Cal. He told me they had given him a car, I don't know the vintage, and that they would pay him $15.00 an hour just to stamp cancelled checks. Marv couldn't make it up north because he was flat on his back just having had one of his many back operations. So he told me, "You have to do something." And I said to him, "What in the world do you want me to do?"

"You have to do something."

So I called up O.J. and said, "Why don't you and your girlfriend, Marguerite, meet me down at the Iron Horse for dinner?" So we met at a table Leo had arranged for us, at the bottom of the steps to the dining room just to the right. And Leo didn't put anyone around us, which was good. They sat against the wall facing out and I sat in a chair facing them.

I'll never forget when I asked O.J. what he wanted to drink, not even realizing if he was old enough to drink. I know they ordered manhattans up so I ordered one, too. That wasn't my best drink but I figured I'd go along with it.

We had a great meal. I don't know what she ordered, but O.J. and I had double New York steaks. After we finished the meal I told him what I thought he should do. O.J. respected me because of my being head football coach at St. Ignatius High School, a team he beat, unfortunately, and I say *he* because *he* alone beat us.

I told him, "Don't be like a lot of people walking around with

your hands out." I said, "Put your hands back in your pockets, go
down to U.S.C., do what they tell you to do, go to class and every
door in this town will be open to you. You'll be worth half a million
dollars rather quickly."

Well, every door became every door in the world and half a
million dollars was essentially a drop in the bucket.

He did give them back the car, which was illegal and went to
U.S.C.

The sequel to the story was, the first time I went down to
U.S.C., when O.J. was about to play his first game, Marv Goux
made him pick me up at the airport. He picked me up in a car that
had enough chrome on it to blind you. Here a future icon is picking
me up. We started driving. I said, "Nice car, what did you pay for
it?"

"Well, I lease it for $50.00 a month forever."

So that was the way of getting around the car for U.S.C. And
so, O.J. basically was recruited for U.S.C. while having dinner at
The Horse.

Batter-Up

Across the street from The Horse was Reno's, a sports bar.
Reno Barsochini was the owner and happened to be a best friend
of Joe DiMaggio. A softball team was formed called "Reno's V.I.P."
Leo was invited to join, and over cocktails at the bar one evening
Leo decided to become a part of this distinguished group. There
were other teams scattered throughout the Bay Area and these
teams would play against one another for fun. Sportsmanlike
behavior was not necessarily followed.

Reno's V.I.P. team was comprised of Reno, Herb Caen, Joe
"The Toe" Vetrano (place kicker for the San Francisco 49ers), Jack
Podesta, (President of Podesta-Baldocci Florists) and Leo. Herb
always played first base. Leo usually played the outfield. Joe
DiMaggio, having retired, was understandably not a part of the
playing team, but would on occasion contribute his services as an
umpire. It was rather a standard situation when Joe would call,

"Ye'rrrr OUT," when Herb slid across the plate, even though he was safe a mile. He loved doing it and Herb naturally played right along and challenged the call.

Whatta yah gonna do? Bantering was part of the game.

The New York Giants vs. the San Francisco 49ers

It was in the early '60s. The New York Giants were in town to play the 49ers in a pre-season game.

While staying at the Palace Hotel a whole entourage of Giants players wandered over to The Horse about 5 p.m., not as a group but in small groups of four or five, about twenty in all. After a couple of drinks they stayed for dinner and then hung around afterwards.

These boys were old enough, but they did have a game to play the next day.

Pretty soon it was closing time and they were still here, drinking and having a great time. Leo was right in there having a good time with them, having learned long ago to nurse a drink. But, uh oh! I hated to imagine what he must have been thinking.

Imagine the results the next day if the entire Giants team staggered onto the field hung over. Such a thing could not happen. But . . . Leo locked up and the party went on.

About 4 a.m., Giant's running back Carl Livingston was not able to stand on what he normally *runs* on. At this time there were still about fifteen players still upright and trying to focus.

It was time to stop the party. With the help of his teammates, Carl was loaded into Leo's car for the long 200-yard drive to the Palace and dropped off with the admonition to his teammates, "Better help this guy up to his room."

About this time Leo was starting to feel guilty, what with the game the next day and all and Carl being a star.

The next day was a perfect fall day—invigorating. Leo, tickets in hand, went to Candlestick Park anticipating a fine day as a 49er fan secure in the knowledge that the 49ers would pulverize the Giants.

He sat in the stands with Horse regulars, Joe Nucatola and Howie Verfall, and when Carl ran for a touchdown, he was surprised to say the least.

"Don't worry," said Leo, "I've got it wired, the 49ers will win."

But as the game progressed, he wondered what was happening to the 49ers. Why didn't they do something? Another touchdown by Carl Livingston. This was getting embarrassing. Leo was perched, elbows on knees, hands on chin, watching, unbelieving, dumbstruck. This was not happening.

After four touchdowns by Carl with goal kicks by Pat Summeral, the Giants won by a good margin, 28-12.

Upon contemplating this dramatic turn of events, Leo pondered, "Maybe the Giants weren't the only ones out partying last night."

Joe DiMaggio takes center stage umping
Reno's V.I.P. Baseball Team.

Chapter Fifteen

BOTTOMS UP

Job Seeking

The turnover of help at The Horse was low but on occasion a position opened up. The following situations occurred when Leo was in need of a bartender.

Vance was a regular at The Horse and knowing that there was an opening, suggested his nephew, Jim. Jim lived in New York, was an excellent bartender, and was very eager to move to the West Coast.

Jim was duly interviewed, passed all the tests, and went to work.

Now, certain idiosyncratic behavior, or acts of God, exists in any town, city or state, and San Francisco is not immune. So it wasn't long before the inevitable happened. It started slowly but the local patrons soon recognized it as a temblor and contentedly went on drinking. We felt the movement, the bottles behind the bar rattled, and soon everything was quiet. No damage. Just routine. But Jim wasn't behind the bar. With the first slight movement, he'd bolted over the bar, raced through the door and never returned to The Horse. Ah, well.

So the position remained open until the next interview.

A nice looking fellow came in and approached Leo. "I hear you're looking for a bartender."

"You're right there," replied Leo, "What's your name?"

"Martin," was the reply.

So they carried on a conversation, each one observing the other. At one point, Martin said to Leo, "I want you to know up front that I'm homosexual."

"Oh, really. Can you mix drinks? Are you a good bartender?"

"Of course."

"Then I don't care if you're pink, black, or purple. Just be here on time and do your job or you'll be out on your fanny. And oh, by the way, his finger pointing to his cheek, just give me a little kiss when you get here each morning."

Martin was hired. He worked hard and all went well.

Martini Marys

Pucci well remembers the occasion of two little old ladies, dressed fit to kill, entering the lounge area and going directly to the bar. Hats were perched just precisely center on top of the head with one lady's hat dipping slightly just above the right eye, rather svelte-like. The other lady was sporting an angry looking long fox, draped across her shoulders, biting its own tail. They proceeded to order the usual martini. Then they ordered another and another until the count was six-apiece. Pucci alerted Leo to the situation and Leo said, "Keep your eye on them." So they continued filling their hollow legs. The count became ten and Leo continued to caution Pucci, "Keep your eye on them." They appeared sober. Their eyes weren't glazed in the least. So when the count reached seventeen—seventeen!—Leo then approached and said, "Ladies, if you care to have lunch I have a table ready for you."

The ladies stood up, straightened their hats, pulled up their girdles, and unbelievably, without wavering, proceeded to walk the three steps down to the dining room.

After a lingering lunch, because Leo was so amazed at their performance, he invited them to the bar and offered each a King Alfonse on the house. They finally left The Horse standing straight up and walking out into the sunshine with Pucci and Leo left shaking their heads.

The "client" in this office reception area looks strikingly similar to the "Martini Mary's" who lingered at The Horse.

(Photo Courtesy of Joe Cotchett)

Chapter Sixteen

HORSE CLUBS

Ladybug Club

Sometime in the '60s Leo had the opportunity to buy 5,000 tiny ladybug pins. Vince Tringali was now in the advertising business and had 5,000 ladybug pins left over from a promotional deal. He didn't know what to do with them. Because they were such a "good buy" and ever being the entrepreneur and promoter and not in any sense of the word *needing* these ladybugs, Leo nevertheless bought the lot. Now this is the creative mind at work!

Leo would accost each child who came through this door, making a big ceremony of pinning this little ladybug on the child's chest and indoctrinating him into the Ladybug Club. A great marketing ploy as naturally the child would beg to come back and the parents loved it.

Those little buggers were everywhere. I thought we'd never get rid of them.

Several years later, on the Peninsula a few miles south of San Francisco, Leo was working the floor at his then restaurant, Woodlake Joes, in San Mateo, when a young man entered and inquired if he was Leo Giorgetti. When Leo replied that he was, the man said, "Well, I know you don't remember me but many years ago when I went to the Iron Horse with my parents you gave me a ladybug pin. Remember? You made me feel really special. I never forgot you." He then pointed to his lapel where, of all things, a ladybug perched. Touched with emotion, Leo automatically opened his arms and they embraced.

The man was at that time a local high school principal, and no doubt he made every effort to make his students feel special, too.

Book Club

Something interesting was going on. I wouldn't say strange, maybe unusual.

For some time I had noticed men, the same men each time, impeccably dressed, arriving one by one and going to the same table. It did not appear they were talking business. They seemed rather engrossed in conversation talking animatedly.

I also noticed that on every occasion one or two of the men brought a book. The book was ceremoniously put on the table. They did not read it but occasionally lifted it up, scanned the pages, maybe read a line or two then set it back on the table.

Someone would flip the pages a little. Then maybe a burst of laughter would erupt. All this was going on while they ate lunch.

This routine continued week after week.

Sometimes the number of men attending varied but it was always men and someone invariably brought a book.

Well, I found out! It started when, over lunch one day, Charles Johnson and a friend were discussing the newest bestseller, a novel. It was an uplifting conversation and took their minds off the stresses of daily life. They decided to meet the following week and continue the conversation.

It became an enlightening event that allowed stimulating debate and stirred them to ponder something besides business.

Thus the Iron Horse Book Club was born and became a fixture at The Horse.

A gentleman from Marin was the facilitator and over time it would include different members. Fiction, non-fiction, political writings, memoirs—all topics were thrown out for debate and discussion.

While their meetings were intellectually stimulating, it was a bonding not unlike a group of women coming together in early America for a quilting party or men from Italy meeting regularly to play bocce ball.

The analogy is the same, bent on pleasure and having a good time.

The Iron Horse Book Club was formed over 35 years ago and is still in existence today.

Wild Game Club

Unique to The Horse also was the Wild Game Club and what was to become known as the Wild Boar Incident.

While Leo wasn't an avid hunter, he did his fair share of knocking ducks, doves, and pigeons from the sky, and occasionally shooting a rabbit from a neighboring field. Leo's gopher-hunting days were long gone. He left the big game hunting to his friends but nevertheless shared in the bounty. Banquets were aplenty and the hunters were delighted to be able to have such an occasion to show off their prowess.

Now let me introduce you to the "Mexican Mayor of Monterey." South of San Francisco, about a two-hour drive, there exists a seaside town called Monterey. Just at the entrance to this popular spot was a motel, restaurant, and bar called Casa Munras. It was pretty nondescript but seemed to have an atmosphere that drew people to it and became a destination, a place to have fun. What force generated this popularity and caused it to become the "place to go" was its bartender, Freddie Martinez. Freddie was a colorful figure and knew everybody in town. You can't get more "everybody" than Bing Crosby or Clint Eastwood.

Having these connections allowed Freddie access to all the local world-renowned golf courses and other hotspots in the area: Pebble Beach, Del Monte Lodge and Spyglass Hill. Every year, Freddie would put on the Bing Crosby Clam Bake in Monterey. Thus he became known as the "Mexican Mayor of Monterey."

Enter the Inner Circle from The Horse.

On occasional weekends, the Casa Munras became their home away from home and they would occupy four or five adjoining suites. Through Freddie, doors opened to all the fabulous golf courses. While Leo wasn't a golfer, he would on occasion join the weekend group that included Joe, Jan, Howie, Allison, Teddy and various others. The hunters would hire a scout and take off into the hills to look for wild boar.

About twelve miles south of Monterey, beautifully situated on the coast is Rocky Point Lodge. The chef, bartender and kitchen help all were friends of Freddie.

The avid Inner Circle hunters, being unsuccessful in finding wild boar, were lamenting this fact to Freddie over drinks on one visit. Freddie boasted to Leo that the boars were prevalent at the Rocky Point Lodge. In fact, he said, they would come to the back door to try to get to the garbage. This statement was met with a very sanguine, "Yeah, yeah, Freddie." But Freddie persisted and boasted to the skeptic audience that he would bring them a "God damned boar."

Therefore it shouldn't have come as a great surprise on a regular fine busy Friday evening, but it did, when one burly Runyanesque character appeared at the main door of The Horse, the *main door* mind you, with a wild boar, dirt-matted hide and all, draped across his shoulders. When this character turned, the carcass would careen around and if you didn't duck, well! It was an awesome sight for city folk, out on the town, to witness.

Now I was jam-packed when he appeared at the door, and I perceive the owner of this carcass was well aware of his propitious timing. Leo wasn't shook up. He laughed and said, "Which one is the pig?" It seems unshaven Freddie looked worse than the pig. Do not doubt that Freddie knew exactly what he was doing.

He was shooed to the back entrance much to the delight of the patrons and the episode was chalked up to another fun night at The Horse.

And the pulse goes on!

Nevertheless, soon a large private banquet was held featuring delectable pork chops.

Chapter Seventeen

HORSEPLAY AFTER HOURS

Pancho Villa's Head

I n addition to Herb Caen I must mention another distinguished journalist who graced me with his presence: an adventurer named Stan Delaplane. Stan, credited with being instrumental in bringing Irish coffee to the Buena Vista in San Francisco in 1953, was naturally imbued with a unique personality and brimming with curiosity. He wrote a travel column for the *San Francisco Chronicle,* which would appear regularly. If he didn't come in for six weeks it meant he was off on an adventure and we'd sure hear about it. One time he came in as usual enthralling those who would listen with yet another hare-brained idea. He was looking for volunteers to travel to Mexico to try to locate Pancho Villa's head. Leo wanted to go, so of course he volunteered.

Forty private planes comprised of sheriff's posses from the west coast of California, Oregon and Arizona took off for Chihuahua, Mexico, sometime in the early summer of 1962.

Once they arrived in Mexico they would take off at daybreak and fly only until 11 a.m. because of the mountainous terrain, and the unpredictable weather. The afternoons often brought thunderstorms and unexpected wind conditions.

The participants in this journey were for the most part professionals: architects, engineers, and businessmen able to take time off for this "South of the Border" adventure.

While their ultimate goal was Parrell, they were to make stops in Chihuahua and Hermosillo. Once they landed they would stay in a local motel, visit the local cantina and just relax until taking off at daybreak the next morning.

A windstorm developed as they were landing in Hermosillo and the plane Leo was in flipped over and broke its prop. No one was hurt but it forced the group to separate and find seats on the other planes. They were able to leave Hermosillo for Chihuahua and eventually reached their destination, Parrell. Pancho Villa was supposedly buried in Parrell, but nobody knew where. Pancho Villa's son, who was a general in the Mexican army, met the group.

He was well received by the men and proved to be an intelligent and interesting host. The mayor, acting as a guide, took them to the crossroads where Pancho Villa was ambushed and slain.

The mayor and the general were apprised of the details of the search and provided a group of local hunters to help in the search. When the group gathered they were told of a $100 reward (believed being offered by the *San Francisco Chronicle*) for Pancho Villa's head. They were to bring it to the square on Saturday morning. The local hunters did indeed show up, but nothing could prepare our adventurers for what they saw: the locals standing there, about 250 strong, proudly displaying over a hundred human heads.

Let's hope the local cemetery was bereft of its occupants that morning rather than a mass slaughter occurring somewhere.

Not knowing what to do to solve this monstrous problem, the general was asked to handle it while the adventurers took off for the local cantina.

Fore!

As dawn broke on a Monday morning at the intersection of Grant and Maiden Lane, what appeared to be large white hailstones were seen scattered about the street, the sidewalks and nestled among the debris in the gutters. There hadn't been a thunderstorm the night before, so what were they?

One Sunday night as on many Sunday nights, The Horse was hosting a private dinner. Several members of the Inner Circle were in attendance.

Two regulars happened to be avid golfers. As Howie and Joe were really getting into a golfing conversation, Joe mentioned he had just purchased a new set of clubs. So naturally it was necessary to go out to the car to view them.

Since it was eleven o'clock, the lane was deserted and it was a brilliant night. So they proceeded to check out the clubs and to practice their swings. Temptation overcame them as first Joe and then Howie teed off down Maiden Lane. As the balls sailed toward Union Square—with, incredulously, no sounds of broken glass—bravado overcame them and they continued hitting balls until all of Joe's balls were gone. Then they started on Howie's balls until they were all somewhere down the lane.

That solves any mystery as to why golf balls were sighted all along Maiden Lane to Grant Street and beyond on a Monday morning.

However, the next morning when our highly charged, but rather mediocre, golfers woke up they were a little chagrined to discover that their night's revelry cost them several hundred dollars. You see, they had mangled their golf clubs to the point of irreparable damage.

I'm surprised they didn't receive a bill from the city of San Francisco to repair the pavement.

Tow Truck Teddy

Here's the best solution yet on how to arrive home safely after a rowdy night. It was the Inner Circle's ingenious idea.

At times, being inside this Inner Circle was the bane of young Teddy Amirro. Teddy owned a fleet of tow trucks under a contract with the AAA. His trucks plied the streets of San Francisco and surrounding areas helping those in distress. Once, out of desperation, he was called by one of his Inner Circle comrades to rescue him after having imbibed too much to drive home. Being on duty, Teddy responded. Leaving his comrade in the driver's seat of the car, Teddy lifted the car to towing position, drove all the way to the fellow's home, and simply dropped the car and its contents off. The passenger woke up the next morning in his car on the street. Once he realized what had happened (he was home safe, he had had a good time and he didn't have to worry about driving home), he came to the conclusion it had been a great idea to call his pal, Teddy.

Word got out. The group had discovered their "designated driver." In fact, since Teddy had other drivers, he soon agreed that indeed, it was a great idea. So henceforth whenever any of the group had a snootful, either at The Horse or about town, Teddy's AAA was called. Whether one had had too much or—heaven forbid—more, they were towed home safely by Teddy and his men, thereby saving the city of San Francisco any further harm.

Hey, Teddy, did they at least pay for the gas?

Caught?

Isn't it the most maddening of circumstances when one wants to be discreet when going out and above all else does not want to be seen by *anybody* he knows, especially when he is across the continent from where he lives and the chances are nil?

Such an incident occurred.

The person I'm referring to is a very well known sports figure, a celebrity if you will, whose name I cannot reveal.

He was not unfamiliar with the Bay Area. Au contraire. He was a student at The University of San Francisco and began his illustrious career in San Francisco. With the bulk of the sports world hanging out at the Horse, he also became a regular and in fact became a good friend of Leo's. To further his career it was necessary for him, after a time, to move to the East Coast.

In San Francisco there is an exclusive men's club known as the Bohemian Club. Just being a gentleman does not gain one's entrance into this private domain. But having lots of money and or being a V.P. or President of some prestigious organization will do the trick. The Bohemian Club is open to anyone in the world who meets its qualifications. Being a member of this club qualifies the member to participate in a member's-only gathering at the Bohemian Grove, about an hour's drive north of San Francisco, during the month of August each year. The Grove is situated on the Russian River and its secluded grounds allow the visitors to participate in group discussions, a think tank gathering, or to take long private walks in solitude. It is a time for reflection and renewal. One can stay a week or two and can derive from the surroundings whatever he wishes.

Mr. Celebrity, as it turns out, is a member and was in the area staying at the Grove.

Coincidently, one evening our intrepid spy, Leo, invited a date to dine at a secluded and enchanting restaurant in Inverness, also about an hour's drive north from San Francisco.

They were enjoying their dinner when Mr. Celebrity walked in accompanied by someone other than his wife, maybe his sister, and was seated at a rather private table. This did not go unnoticed by Leo who was not only surprised to see his friend out here on the West Coast, but trying to dine incognito. Seizing the moment, he asked a passing waiter for his white napkin. With the napkin draped over his left forearm, Leo approached the table *a deux* and said, "Would you like the usual, Mr. Celebrity?" The smile disappeared from Mr. Celebrity's face when he looked up and saw Leo.

"Ah, shit!" was all he could say. They both had a good laugh and Mr. Celebrity's rendezvous was never revealed. Leo, alas, did not receive a tip that night but the next year he did receive twenty free tickets to the super bowl.

Jammin' at The Horse

Eddy Peabody, being the greatest talent in the world on the banjo and known for his gigs in Europe, regularly booked a stint at Bimbo's 365 Club. Most likely there would be in the audience two other talented musicians: Frank Campana, a San Francisco jeweler who was incredible on the banjo, and Ted Balliet, the beat man who handled the intricacies of the mighty bass fiddle.

This fabulous trio would trek over to The Horse on any night after Eddy's stint at Bimbo's. Those lucky few still hanging out at The Horse at closing time, wondering if they should be tottering off home, would soon be jolted awake. The regulars of course knew of these private gigs. I'm sure the word got out.

The doors closed and after feeding the hungry musicians the jamming started. Two banjos and a bass in sync, one taking off, then another soaring, time after time, until finally coming together and reaching a crescendo. Breathless. Then on and on, reaching new highs, until the wee hours of the morning.

And the pulse goes on!

Seeking Pancho Villa's Head—The trip to Mexico.
Stan Delaplane (2nd from left), Leo (far right).

Chapter Eighteen

FREDERICO AND GOD

All of his life, Frederico was a God-fearing man, humble, hardworking and believing in the divine order of his life.

One thing he did not do was go to church. He believed in it but for someone else.

As a child, Leo fulfilled his duties as a Catholic by following the path of all good Catholic boys. He was an altar boy and when it came time for the collection, he would pass the collection plate.

Every Sunday without fail, Frederico would drive young Leo and Maria to the Our Lady of Pillar Church in Half Moon Bay. When church was over Frederico would be there waiting to drive them home. Nothing was said about this obvious transgression, but Leo wondered privately.

This practice continued and when Leo moved away, Frederico still would drive Maria to church and pick her up afterward.

Many, many years passed and as Leo visited his parents often, he noticed a change in Frederico. Naturally Leo would accompany Maria to church on Sunday visits. But Frederico would send eggs, or vegetables from the garden, or some other gift from the farm to give to the priest.

During the week, if he had a particularly good harvest, he would go to the church to share his bounty with the priest. This was very different behavior.

One day, when Frederico was about 75 years old and he had just completed such a benevolent transaction, Leo approached him.

"Papa, what's happened? You never go to church. You avoid the priest, and now here you are courting him with eggs and vegetables."

"Well, when you get my age you can't be too sure," was the response. And with his finger pointing skyward he continued, "I may need a little help."

It was in 1972 when Frederico visited God.

Chapter Nineteen

HORSEPLAY INTERNATIONAL

Sightseeing

While The Horse was a haven for the locals and out-of-towners around the Bay Area, it was also the destination of several regulars who traveled from out of the country or out of the state and made it a point to stop in when they came to San Francisco.

One of these distinguished international guests was Benny Toda, President of Philippine Airlines (located on Union Square) who came in regularly. On one occasion he brought, as his guest, the Vice President of the Philippine Islands.

Another frequent visitor was the Honorable Mayor of Melbourne, Australia, Morris Nathan. Or, since Queen Elizabeth knighted him, should I say Sir Morris Nathan?

Neighboring state Nevada, while not out of the country, produced Senator Paul Laxalt, who always came to The Horse when in San Francisco.

And there was, of course, Speaker of the California State Assembly, Willie Brown. (Who later, of course, became our very own mayor).

I will share an experience with a guest from England. He was an engineer with British Petroleum and one time in the '60s he was in town on business. When he visited me, he felt right at home. In fact, he said The Horse reminded him of home. Now one night this delightful man stayed and stayed. It was getting rather late and he was thoroughly enjoying himself. Leo approached him at the bar and after visiting a while, Leo then invited him to stay until closing. Now, what was he up to? He stayed. They closed. They left together.

The next morning I found out what they did. After leaving The Horse they went on an honest-to-God midnight tour of the city. Since our guest was an engineer, Leo was thinking of all the wonders of the city, architectural and otherwise, that he might be interested in seeing and they proceeded to see all of the magnificent creations of the city that lay open to them this glorious moon-filled night.

First stop was the gorgeous Golden Gate Bridge with its majestic spires playing tag with the clouds. Just to the right of the pay station and down a picturesque drive standing tall is a bronze statue of Joseph Strauss, the Chief Engineer of the project, upon which a historical plaque tells the story of its inception and construction:

> Work on its 4,202-square-foot span began on January 5, 1933, encompassing 80,000 miles of cable wire weighing a total of 83,000 tons. This "Lady of the Gateway to the Bay" was completed on May 28, 1937.
>
> ON ITS BROAD DECKS
> IN RIGHTFUL PRIDE
> THE WORLD IN SWIFT
> PARADE SHALL RIDE
> THROUGHOUT ALL TIME TO BE
> BENEATH, FLEET SHIPS
> FROM EVERY PORT,
> VAST LANDLOCK BAY,
> HISTORIC FORT,
> AND DWARFING ALL: THE SEA.
> THE MIGHTY TASK IS DONE.
>
> Joseph Strauss

Then on to the Cliff House on its oceanfront perch, and its adjoining bathhouses where there was still a smattering of people milling about, listening for a while to the crashing of the waves against the rocks.

A ride up to Twin Peaks where the view from the top displayed the whole city lit up in all its wonder.

Next was Coit Tower, a single pinnacle of light beckoning home the weary traveler. Legend says Coit Tower was built by Lillie Hitchcock Coit in memory of her fireman husband. Standing at the base looking skyward, with the clouds scuttling overhead, it appeared as if the tower were falling.

In 1876, a group of San Francisco citizens purchased four lots on the crest of Telegraph Hill to be preserved as a park in memory of the pioneers. When Lillie Hitchcock Coit died in 1929 she bequeathed one third of her estate for the purpose of adding beauty to the "city I have always loved." A committee comprised of Herbert Fleishhacker, John McLaren, Wm. L. Crocker, James McSheehy and C.E. Grunsky, recommended that an architect, A.H. Brown Jr., be retained to develop plans for a monument to be built on Telegraph Hill. Thus, the monument, Coit Tower, was built during the Great Depression. It was dedicated in 1933.

Our sightseers continued with a drive down crooked Lombard Street.

To conclude the nocturnal journey they took a leisurely drive through the Italian North Beach area past the clock tower of the Ferry Building and on to Fishermen's Wharf. It was early in the morning when Mr. British Petroleum was escorted home to the St. Francis Hotel. It would be twenty years of Christmas cards received by Leo as a remembrance of that eventful night in San Francisco.

Swizzle Sticks

One evening in far off London, a regular guy was sitting at the bar of the Dorchester Hotel. Upon ordering a gin and tonic he reached into his inside jacket pocket and pulled something out. He very carefully removed the item from its container and proceeded to stir his drink. This did not go unnoticed by the bartender, but then again he sees a lot of interesting behavior. Having your own swizzle stick?

But then, wait, sitting farther down the bar another gentleman quietly picked up his drink and moved toward the man with the gin and tonic.

As he started to occupy the adjoining stool he said, "Oh, I see you're a regular at the Iron Horse." He didn't even have to say "San Francisco" for God's sake!

He obviously didn't have his swizzle stick on him or he would have brandished it, you know, comrades and all.

Leo had a way of honoring his "ever faithful, loyal, regular, special patrons." Sometime in the '60s he simply went to the jeweler and had about a hundred gold swizzle sticks made with black lettering, "Iron Horse—San Francisco." A special leather case was also made to house these mementos.

It was only natural, given such a magnificent gift, a token held in such high esteem, that wherever these Horsemen went, they were proud to carry and yes, to display, their very own gold swizzle sticks.

SWIZZLE STICK OWNERS UNITE!

Chapter Twenty

THE 1970s

As the frivolous and fun '50s and the stimulating '60s passed, so arrived the serious '70s carrying with this passage the remnants of the Vietnam War.

The assassinations of Robert Kennedy and Martin Luther King in 1968, along with the uneasiness of the Vietnam War, carried us into the '70s with a foreboding. The '70s were a time of social upheaval, of change, the time when the country was divided between the establishment and the anti-establishment.

Opposition to the war peaked in 1971. In 1972 it was over. President Nixon claimed to have won a "Peace With Honor." Veterans were returning to an unsure life and they did not feel welcome.

The '70s were not a good time for me. Things had changed. People were not coming in dressed nor did they drink martinis. What happened to the glamour? What happened to the pulse? I understood what was going on but it wasn't good for me and

it was happening all over.

With the growth in suburbia, the housing market was soaring. Young people, strapped with mortgage payments, were more apt to stay home and barbeque.

For the ladies, drinking chardonnay was in rather than the martini.

The "pantsuit" for women came into vogue and dress codes were established. A very elegant couple came into The Horse. They were turned away because the lady wore a "pantsuit."

Forget sophistication. Forget our traditions. No need to "dress." Jeans and a t-shirt were *de rigueur*.

Shopping malls and super-markets were flourishing and this was true all over America. The once proud and aristocratic downtown department stores were leaving the cities as the hordes, in their jeans and sweats, found shopping at the malls more to their liking. Downtown shopping areas were becoming deserted, thus cities became ghost towns. Strip malls, fast food chains, fast-paced living, were all signs that the make-up of America was changing.

Mothers were going back to work either to help with the mounting costs of living and raising children or they wanted a career. Our whole experience in living was changing and making way for the future dot-com era.

With all these changes in our living, eating, and drinking habits, I wasn't having any fun. Gone were the City of Paris Department Store and the Martini Marys. I could understand why. I missed the people coming downtown to shop and to visit me. It was time for Leo and I to part.

Chapter Twenty-One

MEMORIES

As with all things, there is an ending. The life here seemed never ending. The pulse! What will happen?

It's understandably time for a change. As the clouds scuttle nervously and indecisively across the skies of San Francisco, so do my thoughts.

I'm remembering . . .

* **The day that The Horse ran out of food.**

The busiest day of each year is the day after Thanksgiving. This makes sense. The people are stuffed with turkey and anxious to get on with the next celebration, which happens to be Christmas. With nothing better to do than to eat leftover turkey, why not go shopping?

One particular day after Thanksgiving 1961, all the throngs must have come to The Horse as we produced and served 660 lunches. When Leo was informed we were running out of food, he ordered, "Close the dining room but keep the bar open. Get on the horn and we'll open in two hours."

Since we were open six days a week from 11:00 a.m. to 11:00 p.m. this was hard to do, but on that day we did not serve food from 3:00 p.m. to 5:00 p.m.

* **The legs on Paula Biagi,** as they flashed out while she danced on the banquet table, seemed longer than her 6'1" frame.

* **The parties in the kitchen on election days.** Were we celebrating victories? No! During the '50s and '60s it was against the law to sell liquor on Election Day so all the bars were closed on Election Day. For the faithful and privileged of The Horse, since the main bar was closed, they simply went to the service bar off the kitchen, where drinks were served gratis with the party spilling over into the kitchen. Of course, those imbibing had already voted.

* **The Horseradish Incident.** A piercing scream echoes through the bar area at the beginning of the cocktail hour, followed by a choking sound. Someone was in deep trouble. As the doors to the street opened and young Bobby Giorgetti staggered out, Leo, ever up to the occasion, sensed the problem, and followed with a glass of water.

After flailing his arms over his thighs and gasping for breath, hovering over the gutter, the story finally came out.

It seems a bowl of horseradish was inadvertently placed on the bar and after inquiring and being told by Pucci that it was tapioca pudding, well, Bobby . . . what can I say?

Other than that, though, Bobby loved being at The Horse. Starting out in the basement peeling potatoes then graduating to busboy with the accompanying privilege of wearing a gold coat. When he advanced to serving hors d'oeuvres at parties, he was in heaven. "Being here was like being at Disneyland."

* **"Good Friday Services" at The Horse.** As was the custom for many years, businesses would excuse the workers for a couple of hours at noon on Good Friday so they could be free to go to church.

A lot of the workforce, including executives, would head for the nearest restaurant or bar to imbibe a little on this holy day. I was one of the many gathering spots. Usually one of the celebrants or two would host the drinks for the rest of the group. Leo II and Augie, being the most magnanimous duo would buy drinks all afternoon, leaving the imbibers in no condition to return to work. The next day paramedics would have to be available for Leo II and Augie when they received the bill.

Each year these "services" were held at The Horse. Eventually the powers that be, seeing that the workforce would return to work ineffectual, ordained that the Good Friday workday would conclude at noon.

* Tom Koewler, the other "Sackamenna Kid". This distinguished gentleman from Sacramento would visit The Horse regularly for his fix: Liver and onions or Mama Giorgetti's artichoke Fritata.

*   *   *

As I think of my once proud edifice at #19 Maiden Lane, now all boarded up, it's hard to imagine the energetic and happy life that existed behind those closed doors for so many years.

As we come to the end of our storytelling I thank you for your interest.

I'll miss everyone and the extemporaneous life that pulsed so relentlessly.

As Leo once said:

> "It was like going to the best party in town every night and
> never having to pick up the tab."

The average life of a horse is 25 years. My tumultuous and energetic lifespan exceeded that to 28 years. Leo sold me to Sam in 1973. I closed my doors for the last time in 2002.

A Tribute:

BY
VINCE TRINGALI

Leo, My perspective and thoughts about the Iron Horse.

I'm a firm believer that any business or team is the personality of the team who runs it. The Iron Horse became an establishment. It was always great. I think the environment of The Horse had a lot to do with it even to the point of lighting. The light made everyone look good and those who really looked good going in looked outstanding.

I have spoken to a lot of people about it and when you sold The Horse you changed the lives of about 200 people. We lost our orientation point you might say.

What always amazed me about The Horse was that I guess one could call it a San Francisco body shop where people went to meet people and it was outstanding. But what also was amazing was that here you have a body shop and within earshot was one of the greatest restaurants in San Francisco. It was almost like two worlds co-existing at the same time. When you crossed the line going into a great restaurant and then you went back in the other way you were in a great social situation. It was interesting going back and forth. It was one of the most interesting phenomena about the Horse in that it had incredible food and outstanding social activities.

I can never forget how generous you were. You would invite ten or twelve of your friends down for dinner on Sunday nights and we would have one of the most outstanding meals one could imagine, like striped bass, chukars, and pheasant. Anything that ran or swan or flew, we had cooked to perfection. Your selection of wines was truly excellent. Something like that one doesn't forget. But another thing about The Horse was the kinds of people who inhabited it: rich man, poor man, beggar man, thief, you name it. Head coaches of major college teams, in this case, Head Coach John McKay, of U.S.C., coaches from the pros, Hollywood movie stars, with whom I had the privilege of having dinner, two-star generals with whom I had dinner. There were just outstanding people there. If you ever had the good fortune to meet the people, that made it even better.

One of the best times I remember: I was on my way to the club around 3:00 in the afternoon and I stopped in to say hello and the whole place was absolutely jammed. There were Leo II and Augie buying rounds of margaritas and champagne, round after round after round.

Also, The Horse to me was a place that really helped my career as a coach. I coached both your sons at St. Ignatius High School and you were really generous to me, and loyal to me. We had our team dinners there. I brought recruits there. I brought the president of U.S.F. there when I took over that job. So The Horse was like a tool for me. A tool for success. And probably for a lot of other people, too.

There were so many fun days and fun nights that it is almost impossible to recall them all. Those were great days. I don't think that at that time there was a more unique restaurant and social gathering place in San Francisco than the Iron Horse. It was just a feeling when you walked in there that this was a nice place to be.

The Horse was a present. And the word "present" obviously means a gift. But when we lived at that time we were living in the present and we were receiving a present by the establishment of the Iron Horse and its owner.

Long-time friends celebrate Leo's 80th birthday.
Left to right back: Vince Tringali, Rick Giorgetti, Bobby
Giorgetti, Leo, Joe Nucatola. Front: Leo Koulos

Epilogue

Following Frederico by four years, Maria joined her beloved Frederico in 1976. Also in 1976, Leo opened his next restaurant, Woodlake Joe's, in San Mateo, California.

Maria died on the day it was to open. Inner Circle friend Joe Nucatola stepped in and saw to all the details of the restaurant for the first four days of its existence.

Sam Marconi died in October, 2001, while living in Palm Springs, California.

Maiden Lane is still the premiere shopping spot off Union Square. The Lane, while no longer hosting "springtime on Maiden Lane," nonetheless hosts its share of activities "en plein air" as with the 2003 Hermes opening.

In 2002, The Salesian Boy's Club (affiliated with St. Peter and Paul's Church in San Francisco) honored Vince Tringali as Man of the Year. The black-tie event was held in the grand ballroom of the St. Francis Hotel.

The Inner Circle is still getting into trouble. It roasted and toasted Leo at his 80th birthday bash December 2000.

Leo has chucked it all to return to his roots in Half Moon Bay. In 2002, a new building replaced the old P.G.&E. Building on Main Street. Built by Leo's friend, Joe Cotchett, a prominent California attorney and preservationist. The new edifice was proudly named *The Giorgetti Building*. This was done in honor of Leo and his parents, Frederico and Maria. The front façade bears a plaque, which tells the story of the displaced Italians during the war, including Maria: "UNA STORIA SECRETA"

In 2003, having remodeled his birth home, Leo moved "home" permanently and lives there presently with his wife, that's me.

Thanks to Maria's foresight, sons Rick and Bobby are blessed with properties right next door. You can be sure that Maria and Frederico are there also.

You can also be sure that the love that existed in this home transcends all time. The

pulse

goes

on . . .

Acknowledgments

To begin a book requires the following: The vision that exists only in your mind, the courage to try to express the vision, and the humility to realize that you may possibly not have the ability to do so.

I have to thank the following indispensable beings who made themselves available unselfishly so this story could be told:

The members of the Inner Circle: Joe, Leo II, Howie, Jan and Allison who searched, and then shared, their memories for those events depicted.

Vince Tringali for his fitting tribute.

Norm Burke, Mimi Barrett, and Johnny Evans for their contributions.

Sons Rick and Bobby.

My friend, Jane Kalkanian (former English and creative writing teacher), the first person who read the original version of *From the Horse's Mouth* and without snickering at this elementary attempt at writing, patiently suggested I delve more deeply into the characters and events depicted in the vignettes. As I progressed, I could see the stories unfold and become more interesting. She was my sounding board.

Diane Thornton, my copy editor who became my friend, I thank profusely for her patience and professional expertise in guiding me through the intricacies of putting the final manuscript together, Finally, I must acknowledge my husband, Leo, who allowed me, and you, the reader, to enter his private life and share his personal memories. Thankfully, he had the retentive ability to recount those adventures that occurred long ago. When he wasn't sure of a name or date, he would contact his archives of friends to refresh. I thank him advance for letting me be a part of the next "chapter".

I thank Mitchell Imaging in Burlingame, California, for photo enhancement. All photos courtesy of author unless otherwise stated.